CRYSTAL

HEALING

Roger C. Croxson

TEACH YOURSELF BOOKS

CRYSTAL
HEALING

Roger C. Croxson

TEACH YOURSELF BOOKS

For UK order queries: please contact Bookpoint Ltd, 78 Milton Park, Abingdon, Oxon OX14 4TD. Telephone: (44) 01235 400414, Fax: (44) 01235 400454. Lines are open from 9.00–6.00, Monday to Saturday, with a 24 hour message answering service. Email address: orders@bookpoint.co.uk

For USA & Canada order queries: please contact NTC/Contemporary Publishing, 4255 West Touhy Avenue, Lincolnwood, Illinois 60646–1975, USA. Telephone: (847) 679 5500, Fax: (847) 679 2494.

Long renowned as the authoritative source for self-guided learning – with more than 40 million copies sold worldwide – the *Teach Yourself* series includes over 200 titles in the fields of languages, crafts, hobbies, business and education.

A catalogue record for this title is available from The British Library.

Library of Congress Catalog Card Number: On file

First published in UK 2000 by Hodder Headline Plc, 338 Euston Road, London, NW1 3BH.

First published in US 2000 by NTC/Contemporary Publishing, 4255 West Touhy Avenue, Lincolnwood (Chicago), Illinois 60646–1975 USA.

The 'Teach Yourself' name and logo are registered trade marks of Hodder & Stoughton Ltd.

Typeset by Transet Limited, Coventry, England.
Printed in Great Britain for Hodder & Stoughton Educational, a division of Hodder Headline Plc, 338 Euston Road, London NW1 3BH by Cox & Wyman Ltd, Reading, Berkshire.

Impression number   10 9 8 7 6 5 4 3 2 1
Year   2005 2004 2003 2002 2001 2000

CONTENTS

INTRODUCTION

Welcome to *Teach Yourself Crystal Healing*. Crystal healing is a very ancient form of therapy, and at the moment, it is experiencing a new enthusiasm. It is also being linked to many other forms of therapy and many complementary therapy practitioners are including crystals in their work. Throughout the ages people have found crystals, gemstones and indeed stones fascinating. They have a magical attraction. Just watch children (and adults for that matter) collecting stones on the beach, the way they hold them, look at them and wash them in the sea to make them shine again. Look at the way that crystals and gemstones have been used as symbols of power and love in almost every society in every age on earth. Also, remember how stones are used to provide information about our planet, our history and our ancestors, through fossils and layers of rock. Think of the importance that space missions place on collecting rock samples to use in their analysis of other places in the universe.

And don't forget, if only we could, that our modern technology derives its basis from one of the major crystals, quartz. A derivative of quartz is in the heart of nearly every piece of electronic equipment in the world. So that every day, millions of people interact with crystal or crystal-related substances at work, while travelling and at home. It is understandable, therefore, that to use crystals for healing work is no big surprise.

Warning statement

It must be pointed out that this book is not a substitute for professional healthcare, if you or someone you want to work with is ill physically, mentally, or spiritually, you or that person should seek professional care. As crystal healers we do not medically diagnose, we are not trained to do so. Medical doctors spend years training to undertake such tasks and they have the appropriate equipment to support their work. Having said this, crystals can work well in helping people with a variety of ailments, and subtle energy scanning methods can help in the placing of those crystals to the best advantage of the person being treated.

It is also worth mentioning that working with crystals may change your life. They are very powerful and can affect the way you are. Maybe they will open up a part of you that has been closed for many years, they may bring back memories and help to remove them or they may change the way you feel within relationships. These changes need not be negative; in most cases they are very positive. If, as you work through this book you find yourself responding or reacting differently, look at the crystals you are using, consider their properties and see if there is a correlation.

Crystal work journal

From experience, and closely related to the last comment, it can be a good idea to keep a crystal work journal where you write down your thoughts and feelings, your results from working with crystals and any other information that you consider relevant. Again, if you feel different within yourself, you can use your journal to see whether there is any relationship between your feelings and the crystals you are working with, or any of the exercises you have undertaken.

How the book works

Unless it is very complex, a book is linear by nature. Learning a new process is often not linear. When using a book to learn a process there appears to be a minor problem between the way we learn, the way the process works and the linear nature of the written word. To overcome this, each unit is, in general, self-sufficient, and if it is not it refers you to other units in the book. Because of this it is important to follow the book rather than dip in and out as you may have a tendency to do. The book initially looks at crystals. It then goes on to show you how to look after you, your client and your working environment. This is followed by how to buy, cleanse, charge and look after your crystals. This provides the background for safe working practise. There follows some work on subtle energy, which is the area in which crystals tend to operate. Then there are several chapters on different ways of working with crystals, building up from simple procedures through to the use of crystals with other therapies, in the home and at work. The final chapter is on the properties of some of the well-used and recognised crystals. There is also a bibliography providing books for you to work with if you want to take any of the topics to a higher level.

One possible exception to working through the book is to read the chapter on choosing crystals, so that you can go out and buy some, then cleanse and charge them, so you can hold them as you read – it's a nice thing to do.

At the end of some units there are exercises; most of these should be tried several times, and can be repeated as a form of revision when new knowledge has been acquired. Where the exercises say to try the crystals and layouts on yourself, it is easier if you work with a partner who can place the crystals on you, and then, at a different time, you can place the crystals on them. After a while, some of the ideas within the units and practise sessions will become second nature and you may even wonder why they were so hard to comprehend when you first started out.

You will also find that some of the work is repeated in following units; this is usually because there are additional factors added, and where basic treatments are enhanced and form part of more complex work. Of course, it also helps as a reminder of the basic information.

Definitions

Some words used to describe various people and objects may have different meanings to different people. Most are used as a convenience. Words such as client, individual and person are used instead of 'the person who would like a treatment', but refers to the member of your family or friend who realises you are just beginning to learn about crystals. The word therapist is also used instead of 'the person giving the treatment', and may be used to refer to you as an easy way of differentiating between client and therapist. Remember that without a qualification and insurance you should not practise as a crystal healer. Other words are taken as interchangeable such as crystals, gemstones, gems and stones.

The book is based on knowledge gained during my life. It has been written without using references in order to provide a flow of information; no books were referred to as it was being written, other than to check my own knowledge on certain crystal properties. Some of the information comes from the ether or from a hidden memory. The object of writing in this way was to provide other people with an insight into the wonderful world of crystal healing.

UNIT 1 – WHAT IS CRYSTAL HEALING?

This is an interesting question and a hard one to answer easily. The basic answer has to be the obvious: 'healing with the use of crystals'. That was the easy part, which now has to be divided up into three more questions: What is healing? What are crystals? How are they used in healing? Some of the following may seem different from what you are used to reading, but keep going and you may see a different way of approaching things. Read it through and think about what has been said in relation to people you know, then reread this section, and see how it can all come together with the problems found in the real world. I am not saying that any of it is the categorical truth, or that I am right and everyone who disagrees is wrong. I am putting forward a way that makes sense to me. It has been developed over many years' experience in many different environments, and from extensive reading, training and discussion. It belongs to no one person and is still changing as I learn other ways of perceiving and doing.

What is healing? Who heals and how do they heal? In some ways there is no single answer to these questions even though there are thousands of books, thousands of courses and healing has been taking place from the beginning of time. Many people may say that healing is curing someone of an ailment or disease by some means. But what if the person does not want to get better? Will the healing work then? This seems to be questions and no answers so far, but the idea is to try to expand the concept of healing. What if the healing is from a distance, someone thinking about the ill person and sending healing thoughts; it does happen. What is happening then?

Medical doctors heal by using drugs, surgery and care; acupuncturists heal by inserting needles at specific points on energy lines throughout the body; spiritual healers heal by using their hands and bringing in energy from somewhere; reiki healers heal by channelling energy and augmenting it with symbols; aromatherapists heal by using oils that affect the body and mind, with body manipulation that enables old patterns to be removed; and so the list goes on. In many ways, when you look at it like this, the healer does not really do a lot. Yes, they prescribe the right drug, find the correct energy channel, bring in the right energy or choose the oil and manipulate a particular muscle – but they do not *heal*. They provide a means of enabling the patient and his natural systems to become switched on and start the healing process for themselves.

The only person who really heals is the person who needs healing. This may not be a conscious decision, the body, mind or spirit may be driving the machine that is the person, but it is the person's own system that actually undertakes the final healing process. All the other external stimuli may well assist that person to heal him/herself, but the final process is their own system that enables the healing action to take place. Sometimes it is too late. Where the problem has existed for a long time or the external stimuli are strong, it is not always possible for the body to reverse the damage and heal itself.

This brings us to the question – why do we need to heal, why doesn't the body do it automatically, why has the system gone wrong, if it has gone wrong? If we could answer this and stop it from happening, wouldn't that be something! The reasons for the body allowing disease to occur or becoming ill are probably many. Unfortunately, we do not help the situation. We subject our body, mind and spirit to a very large number of harmful things, many forms of stress, poor diet, and in the more recent years, thousands of artificial chemicals. All of these tend to put extra strain on the body's functions, which may manifest as illness. Whether illness would disappear if we all lived perfect enlightened lives we can only guess at. The classic New Age statement relating to illness is the word 'dis-ease', and for many who develop illness the root may have been some form of 'dis-ease' at some time in their lives. Often the reaction to a stressful occurrence can take many years to manifest as illness. Until long-term research is carried out, the real cause of many problems may not be identified.

An allied question is: why does the body not switch on its own healing mechanism, why does it seem to require an external source? In many cases it does seem to be able to do this automatically, but if the problem has been appearing over a long time or has been in existence for a long time, the auto-switch must have been missing or somehow switched off by the body itself or external influences, even the same ones that caused the problem. It is an area of unknowns, except one – healing works.

Having looked briefly at illness and healing we will now look at crystals.

Crystal types

Crystals come in many types, sizes and forms. There are many different ways of approaching crystals and there are different ways of identifying them. First, you will find a list of the basic forms crystals can be purchased in. Each crystal type may not be available in each form.

Rough

As they are taken from the ground, there may or may not be points or terminations. They may have a dirty appearance and be very oddly shaped. Unless you find your own or visit an area where crystals are abundant you are not likely to see these very often.

Tumbled

These are rough crystals that have been put through an abrasive process that wears away at the sharp edges and rough surfaces to make a smooth and polished stone. These are used in jewellery as well as in healing. They are now easily obtainable.

Clusters

These are pieces of crystal that have several points attached to them, often on a piece of rock called a substrate. They may be part of a geode, which is a stone with a hollow centre, crystals on its inside and stone on the outside. They can vary in size from very small to very, very large. Common ones include Clear Quartz and

Amethyst, the purple quartz. Clusters can also be double-sided with crystals pointing in all directions.

Points

These are also referred to as terminated crystals. They are naturally occurring crystals with a point on one or sometimes both ends. They have normally been broken off at the base. They can form a broad size range from millimetres to metres. Again, the common ones are from the quartz family, however, many other crystal types produce terminated crystals. Certain types of crystal never or very rarely produce terminated forms, these include Rose Quartz and Turquoise.

Massives

These are natural lumps of crystal which are of a type that has unterminated lumps as a common form. An example is a raw piece of Rose Quartz; in this case, the edges can be very sharp so handle with care.

Cut and polished

These are normally the gem-quality stones used in making jewellery. They can, however, also be used in healing. Some people may argue that their clarity provides a stronger influence, others that they are not natural and should not be used. Each to their own ideas. The stones are normally cut to specific patterns depending on the shape of the setting and type of crystal. The angles between the faces are of great importance, as the internal reflection of light they create increases the brilliance of the stone. The most sought-after cut stone may be the Diamond, which in its natural raw state is not very prepossessing. Many other types of crystals are cut and polished – just look in any jeweller's window to see Amethyst, Garnet, Ruby, Sapphire and others. The quality of the crystals used for cutting is normally the clearest and least flawed and are known as gem quality.

Clear or opaque

Not really a crystal form but the difference can create a certain amount of confusion. The quality of crystals and gemstones can vary enormously, even from the same batch, not taking into account different mines and different countries. The result is that there is a complete range of quality for some stones from crystal clear (it must be where the phrase comes from) to very opaque. The other variable is the colour, by which many crystals can vary a great deal, providing many different colours as well as a large range of hues within the same colour.

The reason for providing this brief outline of the forms is to assist you in identification. Even with good colour photographs, the piece that you buy may appear so different that you may consider it to be a completely different crystal. If the picture in the book is of a clear, brilliant strongly coloured stone, find out if in another form it can be opaque and pale in colour. Although it is partly personal taste, cloudy pale stones may work equally as well as textbook examples.

Crystal structures

This is the chemistry and physics or is it geology? Probably a combination of all and some others. Do not worry – we are not going to spend hours looking at formulae or crystalline structures. However, there are seven forms of crystal structure and they are listed in Table 1.1.

Number	Structure	Examples
1	Isometric/cubic	Fluorite, Pyrite, Garnet
2	Tetragonal	Zircon
3	Hexagonal	Beryl, Quartz
4	Orthorhombic	Topaz, Peridot
5	Monoclinic	Azurite, Gypsum
6	Triclinic	Kyanite, Turquoise
7	Rhombohedral/triagonal	Calcite, Tourmaline

Table 1.1 Crystal structures

These structures can be used to identify crystals and their families. There are other methods of identification that all help. Another is the hardness of the stone. These are graded using a scale of hardness called Mohs scale. This can be used by most people, with broad ranges of soft, medium and hard, which can help when you are not sure about a particular stone. Crystals in the groups above it can scratch a crystal of a particular hardness: those in hardness groups seven to ten can scratch crystals of hardness six and below. A basic set of hardness identifications is given in Table 1.2 (below).

Hardness scale	Standard	Identification example
10	Diamond	
9	Corundum	
8	Topaz	
7	Quartz	
6	Feldspar	Can be scratched with steel file
5	Apatite	Can be scratched with knife
4	Fluorite	
3	Calcite	Can be scratched with a copper-based coin
2	Gypsum	Can be scratched with fingernail
1	Talc	

Table 1.2 Mohs scale

Other methods of identification are really beyond the scope of people without specialist equipment and knowledge. Another simple process is the way in which the stone breaks, that is, the cleavage. This varies from crystal structure to crystal structure, but only works where you can see any surface that has been broken. Another is the lustre of the stone, that is, the way it reflects light, or how bright and shiny it is. It's like the way an old car never shines like a brand new one. Certain types of crystal are inherently shinier.

Can other stones be used?

In general, with crystal healing, we are considering crystals and gemstones which are defined as having a regular molecular structure, sometimes referred to as a lattice. They are not amorphic, which means they do not have a regular repeating structure. There are some stones commonly used in crystal healing that are amorphic, Obsidian and Amber are two examples. Obsidian is a natural glass and Amber is a natural hardened resin. Other stones that are found easily can be used. Some of these are the same as those used for healing, for example Clear Quartz, Fluorite, and Hematite but they are not as beautiful as bought examples. They may not look as pretty but you may be surprised at their power. Ordinary stones can be used if they feel right and are often used for grounding, as their energy tends to be slower.

For those people who require grounding, a good exercise is to find your own grounding stone. To do this go out for a walk in the countryside or on the beach with the intention of finding a grounding stone, and see what happens. You may also want to have a less portable stone to use in your treatment room. Remember that in some places it is illegal and environmentally unfriendly to remove stones from their natural surroundings. If you want to know whether a stone can be of assistance, work through the book until you have practiced the 'Meditation with crystals' and use the same exercise with stones. Because they are denser, it may take a little while to get used to the frequency they work at.

What is a healing room?

The simple answer is any place or space where healing work is carried out. This can be a dedicated room or an ordinary living room used for healing purposes. It can also be outside in a garden or in a woodland area. For example, in the countryside, in an emergency, wherever you are becomes a healing space. Unit 2 gives information on how to prepare your healing space.

One important aspect of any healing space, and especially a dedicated room, is that it is, or becomes, a sacred space. Healing action is often related to the connection to Universal Energy. Later in the book there is information about using this energy, showing that it is not important what your beliefs are, only that you recognise the source and use of Universal Energy. Healing uses this external energy, so many people feel that the workroom should be treated in a more sacred manner than an ordinary consulting room. Practitioners often place candles, images and other items that remind them of their own spiritual connection at strategic spots in the room. They also burn essential oils or incense sticks. Often no one wears shoes in this room; it should, likewise, be used for no purpose other than meditating or similar practises.

What is a crystal healing treatment?

Before you practise it is a good idea to have an idea as to what takes place. This varies from practitioner to practitioner; the basic ideas are, however, very similar. The first stage is a general chat about why the person wants a treatment, they are also told that whatever is said will remain completely confidential. This type of work cannot be accomplished without the client feeling very safe. This is a time for the client to talk and the therapist to listen. A medical history is also taken providing more background information for the therapist.

The client then lies on the couch or floor, whichever is being used. They are made comfortable with a pillow under their head, possibly a small cushion is placed under the small of their back and under their knees. A simple relaxation exercise may also be given, as one of the first requirements the body has for healing is that of relaxation. The therapist reads the subtle energy of the client. This is achieved in various ways, with vision, hands and a pendulum The therapist will then start to place crystals on and around the client, depending on what they consider is required, based on what the client has said, how they behave and the results of the subtle energy scans, plus a large amount of intuition. The therapist will stay with the client. If the client wishes to talk the therapist will listen, but if it is just mundane chatter about everyday issues the therapist may suggest that they quieten or may lead them to a subject that requires talking about. They may also take them on a journey to visit parts of their body or mind that require assistance. This is normally achieved with a combination of crystals and visualisation.

Depending what happens the therapist may change some of the crystals or wait until the end of the treatment and remove them all.

The crystals are normally left in place for between 10 and 30 minutes.

After the removal of the stones the therapist will talk with the client about the experiences they had and then check that they are grounded and safe to go back out into the world. They will also recommend that the client drinks plenty of water and possibly has a hot drink and a light snack to assist in bringing them back to earth. The therapist then completes their notes, cleans the crystals, themselves and the room as necessary.

What is the correct use of crystals?

Each crystal healer you talk to probably has a different view on how to use crystals and the types of crystals to use. The only firm rule that can be stated here is to use them safely, with care and with consideration of the other person. The other way of stating this is that they should only be used for the purpose of good with Universal Love. All stones used on other people should have been cleansed and recharged before being used again. Consideration should be made of the individual and care should be taken not to invade their integrity.

What is holistic work?

The word holistic is being used a lot these days. For work described in this book holistic means looking at the whole person, not just the symptoms. This includes their body and all the component parts and how they are interconnected; to this can be added the emotional person and the spiritual person and how these interconnect and work with each other and the physical body. Holistic work is about looking at the whole person, not taking each part or symptom individually, and looking for connections or relationships with all of the person. It also relates to outside stimulus such as personal relationships, the home, social and work environments.

Another definition of holistic is the connection and joint approach to healthcare by using orthodox medicine and complementary therapy. The idea is that it can provide a greater value to the client.

In particular where diagnosis is required, followed by the use of non-life saving drugs. The drugs may either be replaceable by a therapy or reduced with the aid of therapy or where the drugs are essential, the side effects may be reduced by therapy.

So, in crystal work the idea is to look beyond the symptoms. Occasionally it is necessary to treat the symptoms because that is what the client wants and by reducing the symptoms, other issues may be accessible. Also, if you can assist them in reducing their pain then that is a good idea. However, it is important to point out to the client that maybe they should return for further work to look at why those symptoms came into existence. In general, removing symptoms is not a long-term fix. It is important to assist the individual to find out what brought those particular symptoms to the surface at this particular time.

Intuition

The final part of this first chapter, which seems to have covered an enormous number of ideas and theories, is to do with you. With many forms of healing the healer needs to use other senses when dealing with clients. In addition, with crystals, these other senses are very useful for all the processes involved in selecting the most appropriate crystals. Before you say 'I am not intuitive', try to remember just one example of when you guessed at something, or knew who was on the phone before you answered it, or who rang you as you were thinking of them or whom you rang as they were thinking of you. I am sure that you can find some incident somewhere.

Children, in general, are far more intuitive than adults who seem to have switched off their intuitive mind or being. It is possible to switch it on again and retrain it for our healing work. Many people who practise one of the healing arts find that their intuition increases dramatically. An important thing to remember is that if you try too hard you will not get the results you want. Intuition is about subtle skills, rather like looking out of the corner of your eye in low levels of light, if you think you see something, and then looking as if you do not see it even though it is there. With intuition, listen to the little voice, picture or feeling and believe in it. Aspects of intuition can be like that, a little seed which when you think about it, or try to focus your attention on it, will disappear with the influx of intellectual analysis.

Intuition can also be one of the little voices in your head. The difficulty is separating out what you generate and what is incoming information. When you start to work with the crystals and start to get information about different stones, you have to learn to believe what you hear. It can be argued that anything you pick up comes from within you or is in your imagination. If it works and provides you with information and guidance, does it really matter whether it is coming from an internal or external source?

EXERCISES

At the end of some units, there is a set of exercises, which should be worked through before moving on. For this unit it would be useful to consider one practical and one experiential aspect of crystal healing. The practical is whether you have any crystals already. If so collect them together. Start to consider where you will set up your healing area for your practical work and crystal treatments. The experiential exercise is to consider your intuitive powers. Look at all aspects of your life and try to find examples of intuitive actions. As well as the list in the unit (you have guessed at something, or knew who was on the phone before you answered it, or who rang you as you were thinking of them or whom you rang as they were thinking of you), also include ideas that have come to out of thin air, times when you have known what is around the corner or going to happen next. This can be the first entry in your journal and if you experience any other activities that make you think, note these down as well. The most common is likely to be synchronistic events where several things seem to be connected. For instance, a close friend has also started to look at crystal or energy healing.

UNIT 2 – GENERAL PREPARATION

Of all the units in the book, this one and Unit 3 are the most important. This one deals with aspects of safety and how to prepare your crystals, yourself, your workspace, and your client. Parts of these instructions may seem rather daunting but after a short while, most of it will become second nature.

Personal safety

This is a very important part of all healing and can be divided into two basic sections: first, protection and second, energy usage. There are reports of therapists who train in holistic therapy and start in practise only to get burn-out very quickly. This is often for two reasons: they take on all their clients' rubbish and they use their own energy when treating the client. It is possible to work as effectively, sometimes more effectively, by blocking the rubbish and using the pool of Universal Energy. First, how can the therapist not take on the clients' rubbish, the negative energy they release during a treatment? Within some ideologies, it is considered acceptable to take on the client's pain, which is thought to remove the problem from the client and place it into the therapist's body. This is not a recommended practise. The client can still release their negative energy, and the therapist can ask that the unloaded energy is transmuted by the earth for the good of all and remain safe themselves.

The first part of protecting yourself against negative energy is to learn to become grounded and to remain that way as you work. There are many ways of grounding including eating chocolate, a personal favourite. Others are less sticky! Walking with bare feet is the simplest, particularly on the earth, such as on grass, bare earth, or a beach. This is not always possible, although it is possible to work in bare feet. This carries on from the idea of sacred space in Unit 1, which suggests that no shoes be worn in the treatment room. Next, jumping up and down making solid contact with the ground and feeling the force of gravity upon your body.

Other methods require longer periods of preparation, which give far greater assistance. Try the following two exercises.

Grounding exercise 1

Make sure that you will not be disturbed. Put a 'Do not disturb' sign on the door, turn the telephone off, make sure you are comfortable and warm enough, go to the toilet then blow your nose. Stand with your feet firmly on the ground or if you feel unsafe sit on an upright chair with your feet placed firmly flat on the ground. Then feel your left foot in connection with the ground, feel the earth energy. Different people feel this in different ways. It may be a tingling, or warmth, or heaviness in the feet or some other sensation. Stay with that feeling, concentrate on it while excluding other thoughts from your mind as much as possible. Feel the energy or feeling come up your left leg, this may be very slow to start with, so be patient. Allow the energy to keep moving up your leg through your knee and into your thigh.

When it reaches the top of the thigh let the feeling move across to your right leg. In doing this, it passes through your Base Chakra (of which, more later). Now feel the energy working down your right leg, down your thigh, past your knee and into your ankle. When it reaches your foot feel it flow out of the bottom of your foot into the ground. An alternative is to allow the energy to travel up your left side to your shoulders and then across and down your right side.

If you wish you can keep this flow moving for a few minutes. When you have finished, bring yourself back into the room or wherever you are and let yourself identify any feelings or sensations you may have. Note these in your journal. The idea is that at the end of the exercise you feel solid, secure, safe and connected to the earth. Take a few moments to enjoy the feeling before continuing. In a grounded state it is a lot easier to deal with emotions like panic and fear which is why it is often suggested that

before having to deal with emergencies it is a good idea to take
three deep breaths and slow yourself down to the earth frequency.

Grounding exercise 2

The next exercise is similar and introduces other sources of energy.
It also takes slightly longer. Prepare your space and yourself so that
there will be no interruption. Sit in an upright chair, or at least sit up
straight with your feet firmly on the ground. Take in a good breath
and breathe out some of the stresses of the day; when you breathe
out do it as noisily and forcibly as possible, no one will hear you,
so really push away those stresses. Repeat another twice. Relax as
much as possible and start to visualise or imagine roots growing
from the bottom of your feet down into the floor. The roots are like
plant roots that can be main roots with smaller roots growing off
them. Let the roots grow down into the earth via whatever route
you imagine. If you are in a high building, see the roots grow down
the walls until they meet the ground. Let the roots work their way
through the earth, through the various layers of rock until you begin
to see an orange or golden light. Let your roots grow towards this
light. It might be better to say do not try to stop them as they can
move towards the light at great speed.

When the roots reach this light, they will either try to surround it or
grow into it. When the roots have done either of these, start to see
the energy move up through the roots, in the same way as you may
imagine a plant taking up water. Watch the energy come back along
the roots. The first few times you try the exercise the energy may
move relatively slowly, as you get used to it, it will speed up. Stay
with the roots and moving energy. When they get to your feet, this
time receive the energy in both feet, see that energy enter into your
feet and see and feel it filling your feet up. There are several
sensations you may perceive. Each person feels these things slightly
differently. You may feel a tingling sensation, or warmth, or a
glowing feeling or you may just visualise the energy without having
a physical connection. All of these and others are perfectly normal,
there is no right, or better way, whatever you feel and see is the right
result for you.

Now let this energy work up your legs, into your calves, into your knees and into your thighs. Again, this may take a little time but stay with it and without trying too hard feel the sensation. When your legs are full feel the energy move into your pelvic region and start to fill up your lower abdomen. Visualise it going into all your organs and up into your chest. You may continue to feel warmth or tingling or this may change as you see the energy filling up your body. Let the energy carry on up into your upper body and when it reaches your shoulders see it travel down your arms and into your hands. See it travel back up you arms and into your neck, into your head and face until it reaches the top of your head.

When the energy reaches the top of your head let it out in a fountain so that it cascades all around you, falling down onto the ground. You can keep this fountain going for a while so that the flow into your feet is always as fast as the flow from the top of your head. An important aspect of this exercise is to see the energy or light returning into the ground. You can imagine either that it is going straight into the ground or it is forming puddles that slowly sink into the earth.

That is the end of the first part of this exercise. Maintain your position; visualise a star above your head with white silvery light coming down towards you. This white silvery light, the star energy, enters into the top of your head and starts to fill your head with clear, crisp energy. Feel this energy working its way down through your body in the reverse pattern of the roots' energy. When it reaches your feet see the energy come out of the bottom of your feet and sink into the earth. Again it is important that the energy goes into the earth.

Give yourself time to come round and see how you feel. You should feel more solid and connected to the earth, less fearful and possibly glowing. If for some reason you find it difficult to move after this exercise, just relax and imagine yourself getting lighter until you feel less held down onto the earth. If this does happen it is a sign that you need to slow down, whether you do so is up to you. As you come back to your environment, check how you feel, both body and mind. Write up your experiences in your journal.

Practise these exercises as often as possible. Do not try them when driving, operating machinery or when doing any other activity that requires your attention, as you cannot do both.

Protective barriers

The second grounding exercise also provides you with a protective barrier against unwanted energies. You need this type of protection to stop you taking on board other people's problems and ailments. To enhance this there are various ways to help protect your energy fields. These are certain types of essential oils, crystals and visualisations. Protective oils include benzoin, rosemary, petigrain and geranium. It is important to use oils safely by diluting them in carrier oil before applying them. They should also be stored in the dark and cool. The oils are used for protection either by applying in a dilute form to the skin or on a tissue. The best place for application is the Heart and Solar Plexus Chakra points. These are situated at the front of the body. The Heart Chakra is about one-third of the way up the sternum, and the Solar Plexus Chakra is about an inch below the bottom end of the sternum. For more details, refer to Unit 4. It is important to get expert advice about essential oils before using them on yourself or others.

Crystals can be used for protection by wearing them or carrying them in your pocket. The crystals must be properly cleansed and charged, which is dealt with in the next Unit. Some that can help are Black Tourmaline, Labradorite and Amethyst. As you get to know your crystals, you will be able to identify those that work best for you.

The other way of protecting yourself is to make a cocoon of light around you. Imagine an egg shape that completely surrounds you. This can be gold or purple. It will allow you to remain your normal self but will help stop people taking your energy or your accepting their negative thoughts. Another way is using two clouds, a blue one for daytime and work, which again will protect you, and a pink one for when you finish work and for when you wish to relax. Place your cocoon around you before you start work, before your client arrives. During the treatment, you can reinforce it as you remember about its existence. If the session is very heavy and the client is releasing a lot of negative energy reaffirm your cocoon regularly and keep yourself well grounded. In addition you can also call upon any guides you have or the entity you have as your spiritual being to help keep negative energies at bay.

These various processes are to ensure that you neither take on other people's energy nor give your own away.

Client safety

The next person who has to be considered with ideas of safety is your client. There are three crucial times for them: when they first come to you, when they start to open up and when they leave you to return to the outside world. When they first come to meet you, it can be a very worrying time for some people. This may be a very new experience for them or they may have a serious concern, the reason why they have come to consult you. When they arrive, they will need reassurance that you are the right person for them to see. If you get this wrong, it could put them off therapies forever, which could be a great loss to them. You need to be alert, friendly and reassuring. Try not to be domineering, but make sure that they feel supported.

At this stage you have to leave all your own worries and concerns behind and become very single minded towards the client. A little small talk can help break the ice, but make sure it is only a couple of comments. Make sure their physical needs are met, with a warm room and comfortable and safe surroundings. If you have very strong religious beliefs allow them to show in your room if that helps you, but do not allow them to dominate. This can make a person feel unsafe if they do not share your feelings.

The next stage where the safety of the client is very important is when they start telling you things that are painful or frightening to them. This can even be when you are taking their case history. Their safety depends on how you react. Never panic; if you feel panicky because they have said something that relates to your own life, ground yourself, take some deep breaths and see how you feel. Pay attention to them, focus on them and be empathetic, not sympathetic. Show you understand what they are saying by nodding or quiet positive responses. Do not interrupt unless they have gone well off the subject. If necessary, repeat what they have said to ensure that you have understood and to reassure them that you have understood. This process is a very important part of making them feel safe talking about things that often appear to be very frightening.

The third stage where safety is paramount is at the end of the session, first, to make sure that the client is feeling safe to go out, second, that they have shut down any areas that have opened up, which might leave them in a vulnerable position and, finally, that they are grounded enough to carry on with their everyday lives. After a treatment, especially where the client has been talking about emotive issues in their lives, parts of their subtle energy system may have opened or changed. If they go out into the world where the energy levels are high and sometimes unpleasant, they will be open and may receive unwanted energies. There are two ways of dealing with this: the first is for you to close them down by running your hand down their front, about three inches away from the body, from top to toe visualising all their chakras closing to a safe level. The other method is to take them through a closing exercise. This can be along the following lines.

Ask them to visualise an open flower of the appropriate colour at each chakra. Start at the Crown Chakra with a purple flower and ask them to see the flower closing, protecting that chakra until they wish to reopen it. Repeat at the brow with indigo, throat with blue, heart with pink, solar plexus with yellow, sacral with orange and finally the Base Chakra with red. After this they should be safe, but if in doubt suggest the use of a protective oil or crystal.

If they are spaced out or seem unsure or unstable then they are probably not fully grounded. Working with crystals can be an ungrounding experience. To help them become grounded use one of the following means. A hot drink, some food such as biscuits, ask them to name six of something: six flowers, birds, trees or anything that they are interested in. This acts as a focus for them. Give them a grounding stone, either a normal stone or Hematite to hold for a few minutes. If you are good at telling jokes and it is appropriate, tell a good joke to get them to laugh. As your experience widens you will begin to see when someone is too open or not sufficiently grounded.

Workroom safety

Now, both you and your client should be safe. The next task is to make sure that your workroom is safe. This really means clean from any negative energies that may be left over from previous activities that have taken place in the room. These energies may be picked up either by the client, which may make them feel uncomfortable or by you, which is not healthy. Therefore, between seeing each client, the room must be cleaned. This is dealt with in detail in the next unit. In brief, the main methods of cleaning the room are: to open the windows and blow the room through, light a candle, burn an incense stick, smudge the room or use essential oils such as juniper or grapefruit in a diffuser. As is explained in Unit 3 you can clean both the room and yourself at the same time. If you use a family room you *must* cleanse it after treatments, otherwise your own family may pick up any negative energy.

Preparing yourself

Having made everything safe, the next part is to prepare you, the crystals and the client. As we have already mentioned when you work with a client you need to leave your own problems at the door. There are several methods to help you achieve this. The first is just practise. The second is to ask any spiritual helpers that you use to assist you. The third is a short meditation or prayer. The first means learning to focus on the client, rather than on you. Imagine the client is an absorbing television programme, film or book. You tend to forget all about your own life at these times, so put yourself in a similar frame of mind when you are with a client. Try it with people you talk to or when you are out socially, just focus on the person talking, listen to every word, watch how their face changes, how their statements or phrases have deeper meanings. Also, try not to interrupt, try instead to remember any questions you may have, and the chances are that the person speaking will answer your question without you having to ask it. If not, ask it at a point where they are taking a break. Of course, it is easier to do this in a treatment room on a one-to-one basis, but it demonstrates the idea of leaving all your own things behind. Your spirit guides may be able to help you maintain your concentration, and in a similar way a short prayer, silent or spoken, before the treatment helps put your mind into a slightly different state.

Make sure you are wearing appropriate clothes, not too formal but smart with a professional appearance. White coats are too clinical. Make sure that you will not need to leave the room for anything once the treatment session has started. This means being careful about the amount you drink before you work. In addition, it is not a good idea to consume any alcohol or so-called recreational drugs before working with clients. Both of these will take your focus away from the client. They are your responsibility; treat them with care and consideration. The same applies if you are taking strong painkillers or have visited the dentist and been given an anaesthetic. These change your ability to work.

The crystals must be prepared, that is, cleansed and charged. It might be necessary to do this quickly between clients, especially when you have only a few crystals to work with. Alternatively, it may be that one or two are favourites and you work well with them. Follow the instructions in Unit 3. Make sure that any crystals that have been used and not cleansed are out of the way of the next client. If they were to be close to them or even picked up by them, the client may take on any negative energy waiting to be cleansed away.

The crystals should be easily at hand when needed, but not too close to the client, to reduce the effect of casual response.

Preparing the room

The room also needs to be prepared; the various methods will be discussed in detail in Unit 3. It should be physically and psychically clean. It should be comfortable and warm so that the client can relax as much as possible. If there are windows that can be seen through from outside then make sure no one can see in by using net curtains or blinds. Try to ensure that the room is relatively soundproof so that people can talk without fear of being overheard; and so that there is less noise interference from outside. If you have a telephone in the room ensure it is turned off; if there is an answer machine try to have it in another room as the clicks and beeps can be off-putting, probably more to you than the client, which in turn may affect the client. Try to reach a balance with the lighting. Not too bright, but not too subdued. This room should not be a clinical experience. It is meant to feel secure, safe and friendly. At the same time, it needs to generate a professional image. The room should be simply decorated with pale colours and there should be very few things to collect dust.

Preparing the client

The final thing or person to prepare is the client. They need to be made to feel that they are in a safe and caring environment. If they arrive in a coat, take it from them and hang it up. Offer them a seat and make them feel secure. If this is their first treatment, explain about confidentiality and the process you will take them through. Offer them the opportunity to ask questions when they want to. Advise them that if at any time they feel strange or have strong emotions or anything else to let you know and you will try to help them. Once they have settled, start to take their case history.

Gaining knowledge from the client

This is a very important part of the early stages of a treatment and is carried out for both new and existing treatment sessions, although the questions asked are different. For a new session, a complete history needs to be taken. In your early practise, if it is on your family you will probably know most of the answers. The following list provides an idea of the information you are looking for and why. At the end of this unit is a typical form providing an idea of possible layout (Crystal sheet 1).

History checklist

Name

For identification purposes.

Address

In case you need to communicate; it also provides an idea of living environment.

Telephone number

For communication if you have to change a future appointment.

Today's date and time

For reference; and the time of day can make a difference to how people feel and which meridians are strong and which are weak, which affects the results you may obtain later.

Date of birth (DoB)

Age can affect people.

Occupation

Work or work environment can affect how people feel, as can lack of work or retirement.

Family situation

Married, single, divorced and children all start to build up a picture of this person.

Why have you come for a treatment?

We expect the client to tell us this automatically, but often they do not. Listen carefully as the real reason may be hidden.

What do you think has caused this?

A key question that can often provide a lot of information. If you have any doubt about what has been said or do not understand what they are referring to always try to clarify it, otherwise you may miss the point.

What do you expect from this session?

Again listen to the answer, it may provide more clues as to what is the cause of any problems, mentioned or unmentioned.

Medical history (diseases and remedies)

This may provide an idea of any damage to the subtle energy system. It also gives further clues to the whole person.

Surgical history (operations and physical damage like broken bones)

Again, this provides information about areas that may be weak or where there are energy build-ups. With both medical and surgical histories, do not be surprised if the client does not provide all the information. Most people seem to block out certain things in their lives.

Family history

Is there any genetic factor involved, did parents and just as important, grandparents, suffer from the same problem?

Do you smoke or drink?

As well as providing an idea about health, it can give an insight into social life.

Any prescribed medication, drugs, treatments or medical supervision?

This is where you may get some additional information about medical conditions. If necessary look up any drugs to see what the side-effects are thought to be. This will also give you advanced warning of any contra-indications.

Any other medication, drugs, treatments or supplements?

This is looking at how the client looks after himself. Do they take vitamins and supplements? Together with the question about diet this can provide a valuable picture.

Are you pregnant/stage of menstrual cycle?

Pregnancy is a contra-indication and you need to consider whether you should work on this person. It will also bring up other information.

Describe your diet

Most people instantly say 'good', but is it? Try delving a little deeper if possible. Do not forget to find out about breakfast, lunch and snacks, in other words regular or irregular eating habits. Diet may play an important role in the health of an individual. Other information may be given out, such as too busy for lunch or breakfast, so they make do with a candy bar – not good!

Exercise

This also includes work and domestic situation. A busy houseperson will probably exercise as much, if not more, than the work-out enthusiast.

Sleep

Do they go to sleep easily, do they always wake up feeling refreshed and ready to go, do they wake in the night, and is it always about the same time? The meridian system and the body have their own clocks.

Any allergies?

This can also spark off details that have not yet come to the surface.

Contra-indications

The main ones covered are pregnancy, epilepsy, asthma, diabetes, heart problems and thrombosis.

This provides a lot of information and can be referred to all the time. The next sheet you require is also used for the first treatment and subsequent treatments. This is the treatment sheet. An example is included at the end of the Unit (Crystal sheet 2), but brief description of the contents and reasons are given here.

Treatment checklist

Name

Keeps all your sheets together.

Treatment number

Useful to see how progress is being made.

Date and time

As a record and to see if there are any obvious times of day responses.

How did you feel after the previous treatment?

Very important feedback that may give an indication as to the crystals that can be used this time. If there were any reactions, ask how long they lasted for. Reactions should only last for 24 to 48 hours unless they are actual changes to the person.

How do you feel now?

Gives you up-to-date information; if necessary ask them about any ongoing problems and about any personal notes you made last time, such as an ill child or a visit they were going to make. People like it when someone takes an interest in them, and it can provide more information.

Check appearance

Skin colour, texture, apparent temperature, odour and general appearance. This provides a general appraisal of their current condition.

The rest of the treatment sheet is taken up with a table of crystal positions with details of findings and crystals used. It also has details of any other actions taken, crystal massage and any advice given. A diagram of a person can be used to indicate any grids used around the workspace.

These two basic sheets provide you with a record of the person you are working with. You may think that you will remember things that are said or done, but after a while, you will tend to forget and need some form of reminder. Try to write up some of it during the treatment. Apart from direct information, do not spend the whole time writing while the client is talking. A good time is when you have placed the crystals on and around the client. This gives you a chance to put the crystal layout down on paper as well as any other information that may have become known.

Not writing all the time is an important skill to learn; or rather, remembering what people have said is the skill. This relates to learning to focus on the other person. As you listen, try to identify the important things that are being talked about and ignore the phrases that surround them.

You may like to practise this as a party game. Ask a person to talk about a topic and try to remember the salient points. The hard part is to continue to hear what is being said while trying to remember the parts you feel are important.

Getting the client to speak

The way you sit and look at the client can affect how they respond and, in some ways, what you may remember. Try not to have a desk between you and the client, it is less formal and there are fewer barriers if you have open space. Try to remain open in your posture, do not fold your arms or cross your legs. This again puts a barrier up between the two of you. Try to keep your hands from covering your face as this stops the client from seeing all your expression. Maintain a reasonable amount of eye contact; whatever else you do, please do not stare out of the window while twiddling a pencil in the classic pose used in so many films. You may find that the client will not look at you, so keep trying to catch their eye and maintain contact. When you do obtain contact, provide confirmation that it is all right to look at you, with a smile or a nod of the head.

When they make an important statement acknowledge that you have understood. But again, please do not use stock expressions such as 'I hear where you are coming from', as that will end all communication. A nod of the head, a quiet positive response or repeat in a précised form what they have said so that they can hear that you have understood or not, in which case they will say it again to help you. After which you must again repeat back what you think they have said.

These sessions are not interrogations and most treatments will be for simple problems to start with. Later on you may have to deal with more serious situations both physical and emotional and this is when listening can be of great benefit. Clients may also start to release information once the crystals have been placed on and around them. When this happens they may have their eyes shut, so verbal responses are important. These responses must be short and must not interrupt their flow. If you feel that it is important in this situation, ask the client to look at you to create the supportive eye contact that they may need.

Confidentiality

All the information you get is confidential. It must not be repeated to anyone else. Your case notes should always be kept in a safe place and should not be left lying around your workroom or your living room. The importance of ensuring that your clients records remain unseen by anyone else cannot be over-emphasised. Imagine how you would feel if any information you had given in confidence were to be seen by a third party – not too pleased.

Contra-indications

This always sounds very serious and it is. Contra-indications are those conditions relating to a client that may indicate that complementary therapy is not to be used. As you become more experienced, you may realise that you are being overcautious and that you can, indeed, work with people with these problems. The main ones are listed here with some of the reasons for not working with them.

Pregnancy

This is partly personal choice for a woman. However, great care must be taken not to affect the hormones, blood pressure, emotional balance and the baby. Crystals used on the mother may affect the baby who is likely to be far more sensitive than the mother. Every case has to be looked at and decided upon with consultation with the mother.

With the following contra-indications, the problems would quite possibly respond well to treatment, but there is always the possibility that the problem could be exacerbated. This is sometimes part of the healing process; the symptoms get worse before they get better. The symptoms could also worsen as the energy balance within the individual changes.

Epilepsy

It is not always known what sets off an epileptic fit. If you do not know what to do when an epileptic attack takes place do not work on people who suffer with epilepsy. The client may be able to instruct you. Also, if you do work with people with this condition ensure that they keep you informed of any changes. They may know what feelings occur before an attack.

Asthma

Again make sure you know what to do for a client with an asthma attack. Asthma may be stress related and any treatment that helps the person to relax might be of assistance.

Diabetes

It is important that the diabetic client who controls their insulin level takes a reading before and after the treatment. It is possible for the treatment to change the body's metabolism to an extent that insulin levels are no longer within their normal range.

Heart conditions

This includes high and low blood pressure, physical abnormalities and post-heart surgery. Care must be taken for all of these, each in a slightly different way. The heart and circulatory system is very important and any abnormalities could get worse before they get better. Some crystals can affect blood pressure, in general, red increases and blue decreases blood pressure.

Thrombosis

This is a blood clot in the body, which could move and enter the brain causing very severe problems. Be careful if you work with people with this; try to avoid the area where the thrombosis resides.

Cancer

Not a contra-indication, but a condition where great care must be exercised.

In all of these cases, if you do not feel confident that you can deal with the problem, do not attempt to do so. This is why you ask very specific questions, so that you know the real situation.

There are arguments that follow the line of 'If you are only working for the good of all, nothing you do will harm the client'. In your early work, it is better to take a safe path of being very careful.

Healing crisis

After a treatment, the person you have been working on may suffer a healing crisis. This is where any problem gets worse, or the body tries to eliminate toxins. An existing pain may get worse, or the client may get a runny nose, need to urinate more frequently or some other form of elimination or memory. These symptoms should only last for up to 48 hours. Always warn the client that this may happen, and that it is a very positive sign.

EXERCISES

This unit has covered a lot of subjects, ideas and ways of working. These exercises should help you revise the unit. Take your time over them and try to repeat them several times. Do not try these exercises while driving.

Start with personal safety and work with the two grounding exercises, try them both. Remember that the more you practice the faster they will become. If you find yourself becoming nervous or panicky try any of the other suggestions.

Move on to creating a protective cocoon; try this at home, and then try it if you are in a busy town. Try to identify how you feel and write up your results in your journal.

Practise your listening skills. If can work with a friend ask them to tell you every time they feel you have interrupted them. Look at your stance, where you look and any other aspects you feel are important.

Practise the chakra closing on yourself. One important part of this work is that you should always try everything on yourself first, to see what happens and what it is like.

Develop history and treatment sheets and think about the questions to be asked.

Consider the room you are going to use and think what you would like to do to it to make it comfortable for treatments. If you are using a family room, check the lighting and that any toys are put away.

The next unit is all about crystals, so practise the exercises in this unit and then move on.

Crystal sheet 1   **Confidential**
Name   Date   Time
Address   Treatment number

DoB   Telephone
Occupation
Family situation
Why have you come for a treatment?

What do you think has caused this?

What do you expect from this session?

Medical history
Surgical history
Family history

Do you smoke/drink?
Prescribed drugs/medical supervision

Other medication/drugs/treatments/supplements

Are you pregnant/menstrual cycle
Diet
Exercise
Sleep
Allergies   ☐
Epilepsy   ☐
Asthma   ☐
Diabetes   ☐
Heart problems   ☐
Thrombosis   ☐

Crystal sheet 2   Confidential

Name   Treatment no.

How did you feel after last time?

How do you feel now?

Appearance – first impressions

Skin   colour   texture   temperature   odour

general appearance

Feet position

	Pendulum	Scanning	Crystals 1	Link	Crystals 2	End scan	Notes
Crown							
Brow							
Throat							
Thymus							
Heart							
SP							
Sacral							
Groin							
Base							
Thigh							
Knee							
Calf							
Foot							
Below foot							

Time – Start   Finish

Crystal massage – Starting   Middle

Final

Other action

Advice etc.

UNIT 3 – LEARNING ABOUT CRYSTALS

This unit is all about crystals, how to choose, cleanse and charge them and how to find out about their energies and properties. Remember to treat your crystals with respect and care. They may appear to be strong but any points can easily be broken. Some of the following work may appear to be unnecessary to start with, but as you get used to it the reasoning behind it should become clear. Nearly every book on crystals seems to have information on part or all of the following, which implies how important it is. It does give you a chance to spend time with crystals which is always a nice thing to do!

Buying crystals

The first thing to do is to choose a crystal. If you do not have any crystals, you will have to practise this in a shop. If you already have crystals, you can practise at home. Perhaps before discussing methods of choosing it is worthwhile talking about where to buy crystals. It may be that you are a very fortunate person who has been given loads of crystals, or more likely you are like the rest of us and you will have to collect them yourself. They can be purchased in various ways, depending partly on your circumstances. There are three main ways to purchase crystals: direct from a shop or at a New Age show of some sort; by mail order through a catalogue; and over the World Wide Web from an Internet shop. Although personal purchase has to be the preferred method, the other two may be unavoidable.

Whatever method you use, there are a few things you can do to help you purchase good stones. First, remember that a stone does not have to be beautiful to be powerful. An example of this is Laser

Wands. These are very strong terminated quartz crystals, long, thin and tapered. They do not have nice smooth sides, they are often rough and discoloured and you could easily discard them as not worth having. Pick one up and you can feel the energy. So, do not discount what appear to be rough looking stones, they may be the best crystal ever!

Second, try to build up a rapport with the person selling or selecting your crystals. If this is in a shop, try to work with the same salesperson each time, preferably the person who is responsible for purchasing the crystals for the shop. Once they get to know you, they may be very helpful in simple ways, such as letting you know when a new delivery is due, or buying in more unusual stones. If you are buying mail order, try using the telephone to place an order, or at least talk about it with the supplier before sending the written version. You may be able to persuade your friendly mail order person to describe the crystals they have in stock, or tell you when they are expecting a new delivery. Most people react well when you take an interest in them and their work. Always explain what you want and why you want it.

If you are using the Internet, try short emails about the crystals before you place an order. Try to find an enthusiastic site run by people that have an interest in crystals and healing. If you have web access, join a news group or a mailing list. Introduce yourself and say you are starting and then ask if anyone can recommend a good supplier. Normally these groups are very helpful and friendly. Remember not to give your address out to unsecured groups. One benefit of using the web is that the world is your shop front; the downside is that postage can be expensive.

The final piece of advice with shopping is to be adventurous; if you see something that appeals to you and you can afford it then why not buy it. Make sure you get the name of all the crystals you buy; ask the shop to put each one in a separate bag and label it. If you are buying from a distance ask them to identify each stone; they should already be packed separately to avoid damage. Comparing stones to beautiful photographs can be very frustrating, the pictures tend to be of prize specimens that may or may not look like the one you are holding in your hand. Add to that the problems associated with colour reproduction and your new crystal may not be identifiable!

Choosing crystals

So, when you get the opportunity how do you choose your crystals? There are three basic methods, plus others which are slightly more mystical including the jumping stones and the feeling that you just have to have it. The normal methods are seeing, using your hand and using a pendulum. For this part, the assumption is that you are selecting a certain type of crystal from a group of the same type of crystals. If you are having to choose from a large number it may be better to put a few to one side to work from, repeat this several times and make your final selection from your initial choice.

Seeing

Look at the crystals and using your first impressions, don't think about it, just look – is this the one for me – yes or no? When you have a more manageable number together, look again and see which you are attracted to this time. Use this as a process of elimination until you have the number of stones you want to purchase.

Now look more closely at them and see if they meet any criteria you have set for size, depth of colour, internal rainbows or other interesting flaws. If they are terminated make sure the points are complete and the faces and edges are not marked. Review your choice and if necessary start again. If the shop assistant is looking at you in a strange way, just explain what you are trying to do. Having made your choice visually you may want to use another method to confirm your feelings.

Using your hand

This requires practise to get used to the sensations and to understand whether they are positive or negative. The idea is that the hand acts as a sensor, possibly linking the higher self and the crystal energy, to see if the crystal is the best one for your current purpose. This method can be used for selecting all sorts of things from ripe fruit to playing cards. To start with, try both hands until you find the one that works best. Later on, you will check your receiving and sending hands, but, surprisingly, your perceiving hand is not necessarily your receiving hand. Before placing your hands near the crystals try to clear your mind of the daily chatter, relax as much as is possible and take three good breaths and let them out as fast and as noisily as the situation allows. This starts to prepare you to enter into a very slightly changed state of consciousness.

Next, rub your hands together as if they were cold, palm to palm. Do this for 20 to 30 seconds until they feel tingly and receptive. Put your hand about six inches above the crystals. The crystals should be separate so that you can get your hands over each one. Relax, do not try to feel anything, just let it come. After a short while, you may feel a tingling or warmth or cold sensation in one of your hands above the crystals. If not, move on to the next crystal and again relax, if possible close your eyes and try to keep your mind relatively blank. Wait a few moments to see if you gain anything. If not, move on. If you receive a sensation, put that crystal to one side, and try using the hand in which you had the sensation to choose the next one.

As with all of these types of activities the more you practise, the easier it becomes. At the same time, it is important to remember to keep relaxed. It is very easy to start to get tense if nothing happens. One of the problems of learning about subtle energy is that each individual perceives the energy in a slightly different way. This makes it difficult for you to recognise any feeling you may have as the correct one. One rule that can be stated at this stage is to trust your feelings. If you think you feel something but you are not sure, trust that it is so. If it is not it will fairly soon become clear that you misread the situation. As you progress with your work, the feelings you perceive may well change; the slight tingle from your early work may become a hot sensation that travels up your arm. As these changes take place, follow your intuition as to their meaning.

The number of crystals you are trying to buy may determine how you choose them. In most cases a process of elimination works best. If the shop you are using has any sense it will allow you space and time to select your purchase. Shop workers are trained to be suspicious, so try to build up a good working relationship with them. Having selected your crystals use your hands to pick them up and look at them: are they attractive to you, look carefully at how they change in the light and at any flaws in them that can add to the attraction.

Once you have a few crystals, you can practise selecting them at home. Put your crystals out on the table or floor, sit down and close your eyes. Prepare yourself by relaxing and clearing your mind, rub your hands together and starting about two feet above the crystals slowly bring your hand down towards your crystals noting any sensations as you do. When you are about six inches above the crystals, move your hand from side to side again noting any feelings you get in your hand or visions or perceptions in your mind. Having made your selection try to remember the sensations for next time.

The pendulum

The next method to try is the pendulum. Basically this is dowsing. You could use dowsing rods or a forked hazel stick but they tend to be rather large for this exercise, so some form of pendulum is better. Pendulums can be bought or made. There are many different sorts and many different ideas about what should and should not be used. As always go with what you feel is right for you. The main conundrum here is that if you like this method of choosing you may need a pendulum to choose your pendulum! Pendulums can be made from wood, metal, crystal, glass, rock and even plastic. They come in all sizes and shapes. The best size and shape for crystal work is relatively small – between half an inch and two inches long and quarter to half an inch in diameter. The string or chain should be long enough so that you can hold it with three to four inches hanging down to the pendulum weight with enough available to hold in your hand.

As well as using your pendulum for choosing crystals, you may want to use it later in helping you decide what crystals to use when working with people. Therefore, practise at this stage places you in a good position for later on.

The first stage is to get to know your pendulum. Before using your new pendulum it should be cleansed (see the next section). The safest method of cleansing for the materials that a pendulum is likely to be made from is smudging. Once your pendulum is clean, you need to set up a means of communication with it. As your pendulum cannot speak and can only perform a series of simple movements the best set of links are with you asking the questions and the pendulum answering. The answers are normally yes, no and neutral or don't know. The easiest way to learn these is by once again sitting quietly. This time in a chair with arms so that you can rest your own arm comfortably. Clear your mind and relax. Hold your pendulum in your dominant hand, the one you use for most things. Hold the pendulum so that it can move freely. The normal way is to place the string or chain over your first finger and hold it with your thumb (see Figure 3.1).

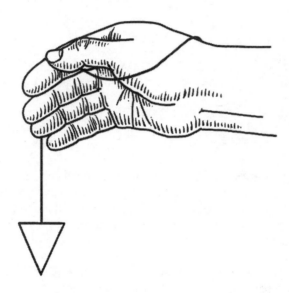

Figure 3.1 Holding the pendulum

Hold the pendulum over your right knee so that the bottom of the pendulum is between one and two inches above the knee. Relax again and ask the pendulum to show you the symbol or movement for the response of yes. If possible, ask this aloud. Keep your mind clear and try to stay relaxed, let your hand be relaxed, do not hold it rigid. After a little while the pendulum may start to move. Keep repeating the request in your mind and let the pendulum do its own thing. It may change direction or intensity over the first few minutes but the movement should settle down.

If nothing happens do not worry. Carry on to the next part and return to this knee later or even another day. Move your hand away from your knee and allow the pendulum to stop moving. Now, place the pendulum over your left knee and ask the following question. Please show your symbol or movement for no. Again, keep the question in your thoughts and relax as much as possible. This time the pendulum should move in a different way. Normally the two symbols tend to be opposites, one may be a clockwise circular motion, and the other anti-clockwise (see Figure 3.2).

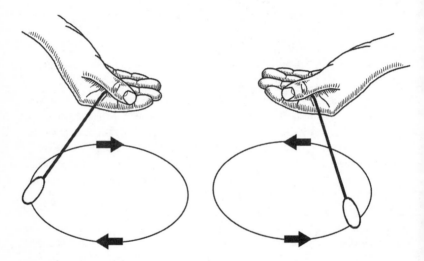

Figure 3.2 Pendulum movements

If nothing has happened at all put the pendulum away and try again later. The final communication is the null point or the don't know symbol. To find this hold the pendulum in exactly the same way with your legs slightly apart and place the pendulum between them. This time you may not get a result. That is fine and a still pendulum becomes your don't know. Once you have your symbols, practise them over your knees until they become strong movements. Then hold the pendulum away from your knees and ask the same questions again, one at a time, until the response is very positive and easily recognisable. Put your responses in your journal, as the movements you have can change over time.

If you do not get any response at all do not worry, it sometimes takes a little while to build up a relationship with the pendulum, or make the connection to your higher self or spirit. Try again later, hold your knees apart so that there is no interference from one knee to the other and relax as much as possible. If this does not work, use your other hand and repeat the whole process. As you get used to working with your pendulum you may go through a series of symbols for your yes and no. If you are in doubt, repeat the initial process. Changes are normal as you learn to work together. You may also acquire other pendulums; repeat the initial learning process but you will probably find that the responses are the same for all your pendulums. Treat your pendulums with respect, protect them in a nice pouch or box and cleanse them on a regular basis.

Now you have your well-trained pendulum you can use it for choosing crystals and for decision making in any other aspects of your life. The only rule is to ask clear questions that can be answered with yes or no. Questions such as 'Which crystal should I choose?' will not work. If you have a large quantity of crystals to choose from you can ask questions along the lines of 'Is there a crystal here that will help me in my work?' Then if the answer is positive divide the crystals up into groups and ask the question again and carry on subdividing until you get your crystal. You may be after a crystal for a particular purpose, such as for use in meditating. If so ask the question 'Will this crystal help me in my meditations?' If you do not get a result, try asking the question in a different way. If you are still not getting a result, the questions are either not clear enough, the answer is not known or there is too much external interference. Try putting the crystal somewhere else and then repeat the dowsing.

Some people use their pendulums all the time, but be careful that you do not lose your ability to make your own decisions by thinking things through.

Practise your pendulum skills on any crystal you already have. You can also use it in fun card games to choose unseen cards, but please do not use it for gambling, as it will not work. With practise you can build up very powerful pendulum skills and use them at a distance but that is beyond the scope of this book.

Other ways of choosing

Those are the three main ways of choosing crystals – by vision, hand, and pendulum. Other people develop their own ways including if the crystal is still in the shop in a week they will buy it. This is particularly good for very expensive stones. It is also possible just to ask a crystal if it is right for you, or to ask it if it wants to come with you. While selecting crystals, you can also ask it what purpose it will play in your life. Some crystals come to you for different reasons. Some for helping keep your room in good condition, some for meditation, some for giving away and some for healing, either you or those you are working on. Occasionally you may see a crystal that just jumps straight out at you, or appears to. This is a good sign that you should consider acquiring that particular crystal.

Sending and receiving hands

You may already know which of your hands acts as a receiver and which acts as a sender. If you have yet to find out try the following exercise. You will need two Clear Quartz points. The first stage is to use one point, place it in your right hand with the point towards the fingers, relax, and let your mind go quiet. How does it feel? Is it comfortable or unpleasant? If it is comfortable, place the crystal in your other hand with the point towards the wrist. How does this feel? Again, if it is comfortable place the second crystal in your right hand with the point towards the fingers. This completes a circuit from the receiving hand to the sending hand. If this feels comfortable, although to start with it may feel strange, then your receiving hand is your left hand and your sending hand is your right hand.

If any of these trials have felt uncomfortable, even to the extent of shooting pains through the arm, then you need to try the reverse pattern with the crystal pointing towards the fingers in the left hand and the crystal towards the wrist in the right hand. If this then feels comfortable, your receiving hand is your right hand and your sending hand is your left hand. Occasionally the crystals you are using may be receiving and sending crystals. If neither of these ways works try changing the crystals over and starting again. Your receiving and sending hands will be whichever way round is comfortable.

Cleansing

This stage is of the utmost importance. Working with dirty crystals is like eating with dirty plates, you may get ill. This sounds a bit dramatic but crystals carry energy, act as a transducer, and transmit energy. This cleansing is not to do with making them physically clean, although you may wish to do that as well. Some physical dirt may be ingrained in the crystal, for instance, Madagascan Quartz may have red earth on it which stains the clear quartz a pink-brown colour. Even if the crystal is soaked and scrubbed it will not get rid of that colour. The cleansing in this section is all at the subtle energy level. When you first get a crystal, you do not know where it has been or what it has been through. Therefore, it is very important that you help the crystal to discharge any negative energy it may have collected.

Sometimes when you are given a crystal you may know it comes with love and you may not want to clean it. That is fine as long as the person giving it to you has cleansed it and then recharged it. Crystals need to be cleansed on a regular basis. Each time you get new stones they should be cleansed; every time they are used for healing they should be cleansed. Crystals in your healing room environment should be cleansed very regularly as should any jewellery that you wear, particularly any you wear when working with people. The same applies to jewellery you wear out in busy places such as work, shops and communal areas. So, keep your crystals cleansed!

Not all crystals can be cleansed in the same way. Some will be damaged by salt or water. In general, the harder the crystal the more impervious it is to damage, but there will always be exceptions. Be careful when cleaning clusters as the base on which the crystals have grown may be of a much softer material than the crystals themselves. The most general form of cleansing is with smudge. This is a personal favourite for many reasons, including the actions and the space it creates. The nice thing about smudge is that as well as your crystals it will also cleanse you and your room. The type of cleansing also depends on what has happened to the crystal or what it has been used for. The heavier the work, the stronger the cleansing the crystal will need. The more traumas the crystal has been subjected to, in mining and preparation, the greater the cleansing it will require. Some forms of cleansing will provide a deeper cleansing than others; they may also take longer.

Smudging

What is smudge and where does it come from? Very simply, smudge is the burning of herbs and the use of the smoke to remove negative energy. Smudge has been used in many forms by a wide variety of cultures throughout time and the world. Many people relate smudge to the Native North Americans who use it in their ceremonies and in healing. It is also used in Europe with slightly different herbs. One of those herbs is the same as used in Chinese acupuncture, mugwort. Many other countries burn herbs for cleansing: incense in India, herbs in parts of Africa and even in the Christian Church. Some of these actions have become ritualised and seem to have lost part of their original meaning, but their basis is to use smoke to clear away negative energy.

The smudge used for cleansing crystals uses three or four dried plants including sage, cedar, lavender, sweetgrass, mugwort and ladies' bedstraw. The last two are European while sweetgrass is from America. Although there is a difference in the sages from the USA and UK, both work equally well. Smudge is normally obtainable in either a bound stick, which is burnt from one end or as a mix that is placed in a fireproof dish, lit and kept smouldering. What you use is personal choice. Smudge is normally available from New Age shops or the same outlet that you obtain your crystals from.

The use of smudge can be developed into a ritual. It requires a fireproof dish, smudge mix or a smudge stick, matches and a wafting device such as a large feather. The burning of smudge can be describe as bringing together the four natural elements: fire, water, air and earth. Some people may disagree with this but I feel it is an important connection to nature. One container that can be used for burning smudge is a large shell – some say an abalone. The connections to the elements are as follows: fire is the burning herb, water is the shell, air is the rising smoke, and earth is the herb itself. As most crystals come from the earth, the link to the four elements seems to bring a holistic element to the act of cleansing. The wafting device to move the smoke around can be a piece of card or a feather or even a bird wing, preferably from a road kill which makes good use of a tragedy.

Have ready the crystals that need cleansing, place your loose smudge mix in the dish or shell. If you are using a smudge stick loosen the burning end (normally the end with thinner sticks and less binding) so that the air can get into it. Use a match to light the smudge and let it burn, then waft it to generate smoke; keep wafting to keep it smouldering. Hold each crystal in the smoke for as long as you feel is sufficient (see Figure 3.3). Alternatively, if you have several crystals that only require a light cleansing then waft the smoke over them. When you have finished smudging your crystals, you can walk around the room wafting the smoke into the corners, up to the ceiling and down to the floor. Remember it is smoke and will trigger any smoke alarms.

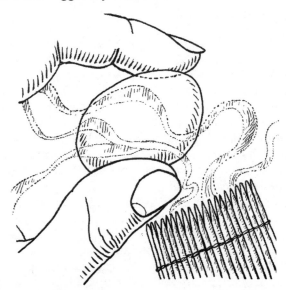

Figure 3.3   Smudging

Finally, you can smudge yourself or you can smudge yourself first. It is easier if you have someone smudge you. Work from the feet to the head, up the front and down the back, under the arms and feet. By smudging the room and yourself, you will remove any negative energy left from the person you have been working with. You learn to recognise this energy but not take it in. Sometimes when you return to your healing room the atmosphere feels like a thick soup; this must be cleaned away and transmuted to positive energy.

Smudge can also be used after an argument to clear the room or the house. After physically cleaning the house, go around with the smudge. Some people do not like the smell of smudge. I was once teaching an adult education class in the evenings, using lots of smudge and each week the class teacher left a message asking me not to use that revolting smelling substance, and this was in a class that stank of socks and sweat. Each to his own! Finally make sure the smudge is not still burning before leaving it. As they say, do not leave burning things unattended. Also, be careful of smudge and candles when you are meditating; ensure they will not fall over or, if you fall asleep, that you will not fall onto them.

Salt water cleansing

Smudge can be used on all types of crystals with no harm, but it is not the strongest of cleansing methods. The next method may provide a deeper energy cleansing but it can only be used on hard non-porous crystals such as the quartz family. If some crystals are left in water or salt water they will be damaged, for instance Calcite, Turquoise, Rhodochrosite and Fluorite clusters. This is only a short list and is not comprehensive. If in doubt – don't. The method is to immerse the crystals in a saline solution. You will need a clear glass bowl, salt (preferably natural sea salt) and clean water, preferably from a natural source. Natural salt, sea salt or untreated rock salt is preferred as there are no added chemicals to aid in keeping the salt flowing. It does not matter if the salt is sticky, as it will be added to the water to form a solution. Natural water from springs or wells, especially holy wells and springs is preferred for two reasons. First, it has not gone through the cleaning process that tap water is subjected to, it has filtered through the ground in a natural way. There is the problem now of chemical run-off but it is normally less polluted than tap water. You may be lucky and get your water from a very old source of an underground water store, which will be pollutant free. The second reason is that the energies from a sacred site will add to your cleansing, crystals and your work. However, only obtain water from these sites if it is acceptable to those that run them or on whose land they exist. If you cannot get water from these sources then do use tap water. For some it is the only water available.

The glass bowl will need to be large enough to take your crystals and for them to be well covered by the saline solution. Half fill the bowl with your water, pour in some of the salt and swirl it around so that it all dissolves. Remember that if you put too much salt in it will not all dissolve. Try the equivalent of two dessertspoons to half a pint of water. If there is a little salt left it is not important. Now place your crystals in the salt solution. Be careful of those with points so that they do not bang on the glass or on any other crystals. How long the crystals remain in the salt water depends on two things. First, how and what they have been used for, and second on how you feel about them, whether they feel to you to be energetically clean. As a rough guide they should be left for at least an hour and maybe up to 24 hours. If the usage is very light then just a swirl around in the salt water may be enough.

When the crystals are taken out of the salt water, they need to be rinsed in fresh water to remove the salt from them. If possible, use the same sourced water as before, but if that is not available, rinsing them under a running tap will work. Then let them dry or dry them with a soft cloth.

Water cleansing

Crystals can also be cleansed in water, preferably running water like a stream. Again, if necessary water from running taps will work. Water cleansing will work for lightly used stones. Not all crystals appreciate water. Be careful of soft stones including Turquoise, Azurite, Calcite, Fluorite and some crystal clusters.

Salt cleansing

Crystals can be cleansed in loose salt, rather like preserving vegetables. In a suitable container place a layer of salt, place your crystal on this layer and cover it completely with salt and leave it for as long as you consider necessary. As before, it depends on what the crystal has been used for. Where great emotional distress has been uncovered then it may take many days or weeks for the stone to be cleansed. If possible, cover the container to stop it filling up with dust and to reduce the absorption of water by the salt. This method is best for hard impervious stones.

Earth cleansing

For those stones that have had to work hard, they may need to go back to Mother Earth for their own healing. If you just bury a crystal, you may never see it again. Therefore, to safeguard your crystals try the following method. This time the tools are a clay or terracotta flowerpot, some earth from wherever you are going to bury your crystal, a hole in the ground where you are going to bury your crystal and a means of marking the ground where the crystal is buried, like a stick or pile of stones.

Half fill the flowerpot with the soil, place the crystal on the soil and fill the flowerpot to the top with more soil. Dig a hole in the ground large enough to take the pot so the top of the pot is about a foot below the surface. Place the pot in the hole and cover with soil and mark where it is. After a few months you may want to check on your crystal, dig up the pot, get the crystal out and rinse off the dirt. How does it feel? By the time you are doing this you will understand about perceiving the energies of crystals, as a complete cleansing could take at least a year! If you feel the stone has been fully cleansed, keep it out; if not refresh the earth in the pot, replace the crystal, rebury and mark it. Test the crystal again in a few months' time.

Breath cleansing

A very fast and easy method of cleansing crystals is using your own breath. You just blow on the crystals. First, clear your mind as much as possible, then hold the crystal in your fingers and gently blow on it, thinking of removing any negative energy. As the negative energy is removed visualise its being absorbed by the ground and being transmuted into positive energy for the greater good of all. This works well on stones that have been used briefly or for gentle and quick treatments or where you only have a few crystals available but several people to work on in quick succession.

Sound cleansing

The final method of cleansing is the use of sound. Bells, tuning forks, Tibetan bowls or other reasonably pure sound producers can be used. Apart from the Tibetan bowl, place the crystals near the sound source and produce the sound. With the Tibetan bowl, the crystal can be placed in the bowl and the bowl made to sing. Be careful of terminated crystals in the singing bowl, as they do tend to move around and the point can be chipped.

Those are the main methods of removing negative energy from your crystals. Try as many as possible. There may be one or two methods that really appeal to you; if they are appropriate adopt them, you can always change your methods later. As mentioned at the beginning, my own favourite is smudging, followed by sound with a Tibetan singing bowl. I like the procedures associated with these two methods.

Energy charging

Now your crystals are energetically clean and any negative energy removed they will need to be charged with energy of your choice. This is not programming the crystals but offering them a replacement for the negative energy that has been removed. The type of energy you use may affect the way the crystal works. The main sources of energy are the sun, the moon, reiki, breath, running water and even thunderstorms. Although the crystal has its own energy, the charging energy helps the crystal work and supplies the crystal with its own source of energy. For instance, in our culture, we consider the moon feminine, watery, and emotional and crystals that are charged in the light of the moon have a gentle way of working with their own energy, whereas the sun is male and fiery, and gives a more dynamic approach to the crystals work. These influences are very subtle.

Try to decide which form of energy you want to work with and charge your crystals accordingly.

The moon, as just mentioned, is considered to be female, watery, gentle, kind, emotional and deep and cool. You may want to use a particular phase of the moon. This is best for the initial charging; otherwise, you may not have enough crystals to last the 28 days between similar phases!

The sun is hot, fiery, dynamic, male, active, energising, fast and slightly pushy.

Reiki can be used to charge crystals and this gives them the energy and approach of the reiki masters and mistresses.

Breath can be used to charge crystals. When blowing on them hold in your mind the intent you want the crystal to take. It may be as simple as 'for the good of all', or to 'provide caring healing' or whatever you wish. Crystals do not like negative intentions so they will not work or may only backfire on the person who uses them.

Placing crystals by running water will provide them with a flowing, bright, chirpy energy that is also refreshing from the negative ions given off by the splashing water.

Finally, thunderstorms could be used for charging crystals, but think of the energies involved! Of course, all of your crystals may be affected by a thunderstorm, but the two parts of the storm will tend to equal out. The heavy, headachy and hot build-up is counteracted by the coolness and clear air that comes after the storm breaks and the rain begins.

So, take your pick, try several and see if you can feel the difference. To charge a crystal, place it in the energy of your choice. This can be outside but if that is not possible use a windowsill or a shelf that gets the sun or moonlight. Leave them for about 24 hours. If you want, they can be left in both sun and moon. If you use a stream, beware of the affinity of crystals to Mother Nature, in that the crystals like to return to their home by jumping into the stream. It may be advisable to place them under some protection, and if they are stones that do not like water, such as Turquoise, make sure they remain dry.

At this stage you will have selected, cleansed and charged stones ready to be put to use. However, the question is to what use can this crystal be put, and what does each crystal do?

Finding out what each crystal does

There are several ways of finding out. The simplest, but not the best, is to read about the stones in a book. The last unit of this book provides a basic idea about the powers of a small group of crystals, but those are not necessarily your ideas or those of your crystal. They may be similar, but not the same. So, try not to use written form first. The best way is to try to get as much information as possible from the crystal itself. This can be achieved in a variety of ways.

Holding the crystal

The first is to hold the stone in your hand, try to clear your mind of everyday activity and see what comes to you. Allow your intuition to connect with the crystal. You may get a picture, a message or a feeling as to the purpose of the crystal. You can then ask questions, which may assist in increasing your knowledge and connection to this particular crystal. Questions such as 'Are you to help me in my healing work?' or 'Have you come to help me meditate', any question that you feel is important to you. Of course, the crystal may not answer, or it may answer in an indirect way by showing you a picture, a dream like sequence, or even an unusual feeling somewhere in your body.

Crystal meditation

The next level of obtaining information about the crystal is to undertake the same sort of exercise but instead of just holding the crystal, use it as part of a meditation. This requires more time and perhaps preparation, which is worthwhile, as it should provide a deeper understanding of your crystal. Make sure you will not be disturbed, take the phone off the hook, set up your altar, if you have one, light a candle, make yourself comfortable and relax, clearing your mind. Hold the crystal in cupped hands or between your two hands as if holding something precious. Start your normal meditation process of a mantra or breathing, and once you have started to meditate ask the crystal to tell you about its powers and purpose. When you have finished your meditation, write down as much as possible. The answer you get may not be direct. You may get pictures, a message, a symbol, a scent even. You may wish to stop the first meditation at this stage and return to it again later to include the next part.

The next stage during meditation is to ask to see the diva for the crystal. There are at least two divas for each crystal. The first is the overall diva for that particular type of crystal and the second is the diva for that actual stone. The overall diva that you connect with may be for the type of crystal for the region where it comes from, or for all places in which the crystal is found. The diva is the spirit, the spiritual memory of the crystal. It is the soul source for the crystal, which contains information about the powers of the stone. The diva may come to you in many forms, a picture, words, an allegory or even a puzzle. In your meditation, ask the crystal's divas to show themselves to you. When they do, you can ask questions and you should get answers. Again, at the end of the meditation write down your findings, it is always surprising how little can be remembered after an hour, but then that is an excuse to meditate again.

Living with crystals

The next practical way of finding out about the crystal is to try it on yourself. This is in two parts: the first is to place the crystal on your body and the second is to keep the crystal with you for a week – day and night. For the first part, allow yourself time and space and lie down and hold the crystal. Clear your mind and see if there is anywhere on your body the crystal should be placed. If nothing comes to you, place your hands and the crystal over your Heart Chakra. Try to keep your mind as clear as possible and pay attention to your physical, emotional and spiritual feelings. After a few minutes, you may notice a change in your feelings or a sensation in your body. Keep a mental note of these. After 20 minutes come back to this world and write down your findings. Any sensations you perceived may have come from the crystal and you now know what the crystal can do. You will have to apply this knowledge, sometimes by thinking about the symptom and then finding a crystal that works for that symptom. For instance, if the crystal gave a warm sensation it can be used where the body is cold or possibly for something like poor circulation.

The second part to this exercise is to keep the crystal with you 24 hours a day. Live, breath, sleep with this crystal. Try to note any changes in yourself. These may be physical improvements or degradations, emotional changes or spiritual connections. Try to recall your dreams, as they may have information for you. It may be that you notice that you have more dreams or fewer dreams. You may sleep better or worse. You may wake feeling more refreshed or tired. Write your feelings down, even if you think that there is no relationship to the stone. Carry on your normal life, but try not to take alcohol or recreational drugs as these may interfere with the crystal. After a week thank the crystal and look at your findings. If you find that your sleep pattern is too deranged, carry the stone only during the day.

Now that you have your own knowledge of the crystal, you may want to refer to other people's ideas about this particular type of crystal. Remember that your ideas are the best ones for your crystals. Whatever the result you should now have a good connection to this crystal. Like all new skills, it takes a long time to build up a good knowledge of the working tools. A crystal course normally takes upward of two years to complete, so a week for each crystal is not long. Having lived with one crystal, give yourself a break before starting on another one. Later in the book, there is information about the beginning set of crystals. If you want, start with the following exercises using Clear Quartz, Rose Quartz and Hematite. The Clear Quartz should be terminated and the Rose Quartz should be lightly pink and as transparent as possible and the size of a large peach stone. The Hematite should be shiny silver and about the same size as the Rose Quartz.

EXERCISES

The exercises for this unit are to carry out everything that has been discussed that you feel is applicable to you. This will take several weeks to complete; it is worthwhile repeating the exercises until you feel confident with them.

Start with choosing a crystal and learning to use a pendulum; try the different methods in the privacy of your own home, if possible, before venturing out.

Move on to cleansing. Try the salt water and smudging techniques, if you are using Clear Quartz, Rose Quartz, but if using Hematite do not put it in salt water, only use the smudge.

Charging your crystals with moon and sun energies

Finally, try all of the exercises for finding out about your crystals. If you have more than one of a type, you do not have to live with each one, but it can be interesting to hold them and meditate with them to discover any differences between them. Keep a good record of all your work, as it can be useful to refer to when wondering which crystals to use. Enjoy meeting your crystals, have fun with them and remember – believe in your intuition.

UNIT 4 – CHAKRAS AND AURAS

In this unit we are going to look at a major aspect of what has become known as subtle energy. Crystal healing can help with physical problems by working on the body at a much higher level than direct manipulation. By using the higher vibrations of crystals, it is possible to get nearer to the possible real cause of the manifest problem.

The subtle body

The chakras and auras are the entry points that we can use to access the subtle energy of the person. Other methods of accessing the subtle body that you may come across include the meridian system from traditional Chinese medicine. Meridians are a series of channels in the body that enable energy to flow from one part of the body or one organ to another. They have a specific order and each meridian is more active at certain times of day. On each meridian, there are very specific points that can be used to stimulate or reduce the energy flow through the meridian. The objective is either to release a blockage or slow down the flow of energy at these points, making the energy flow normal and reducing the symptoms caused by incorrect flow. Either pressure or very fine needles usually achieves this. Burning herbs which heat the meridian point is another ancient method and in the last few years lasers have also been used.

Chakras are becoming recognised in the west. They have been known in the east, India and China, for a very long time. It is possible that they were identified in India and several thousand years ago taken to China and Japan and included in the healing methods there. The other possibility is that they were discovered in both the east and India. The word chakra comes from the Sanskrit for wheel. This is only part of the story, as 'wheel' tends to indicate a circle. Those people that can see chakras or trace them consider that they are more like a vortex than a wheel.

The narrow end is nearer the body and the open end is away from the body. However, they are not separate from the body, they are an entry point to the body for subtle energy and meet with various glands and nerve systems. Each chakra has a variety of factors associated with it. Among others, there are colours, sounds, gods and goddesses, nerve systems, glands, body parts and the elements. For our work, we are interested in the various connections within the body and associated colours.

We are going to work with the seven main chakras (see Figure 4.1); there are however, many other chakras throughout the body. These are the secondary and tertiary chakras. They are much smaller, but

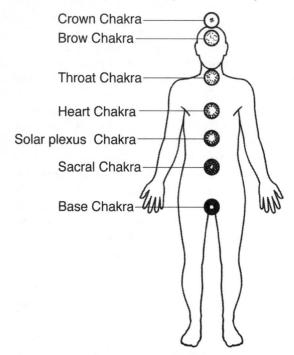

Figure 4.1   The seven chakras

some of them are equally important for healing. For instance, those in the palms of the hand may have something to do with the way we feel energy from our crystals and from other people. One view is that each specific point on each meridian is also a very small chakra indicating that there are hundreds of them throughout the body. It is possible that one day we will have sufficient information to understand the subtle energy system fully, but until then, we can only see what works for each of us.

The seven main chakras

Chakra 1

The chakras are normally numbered from the base up to the top. The first chakra is known as the Base Chakra and is located low in the body in between the anus and the genitals. This chakra relates to the survival of the individual and helps keep the person stable and grounded, down to earth. The open end of the energy vortex is directed downwards towards the earth helping to make the grounding connection. The related gland is the adrenal gland, otherwise known as the fight or flight gland. The adrenal gland helps a person survive in times of emergency as it changes the metabolism of the body. So that when either running away from danger or standing and facing it, non-essential systems in the body either slow down or stop and essential systems are more active. For example the digestive process is stopped as it is not needed on a temporary basis and the circulatory process is increased to deliver more energy to the muscles. The digestive mechanism serves no short-term purpose; all energy used will be that stored within the body. The muscles need as much food and oxygen as possible so the blood has to be pumped around the body at a faster rate.

The colour associated with the Base Chakra, in the west, is red. Red is a very vibrant, physical colour, and has the longest wavelength and slowest vibration of the visible spectrum. It encourages action from people at a very physical level. It can also be very warming and in too great a volume, it may even lead to violence. If you want a restful room, do not use red paint. However, there can be many other colours associated with the Base and the other chakras. The Base Chakra is sometimes considered to be connected with survival because it is near the genitals, and therefore linked to procreation. It is possible that there is a difference between chakras and the sexes, as the Base Chakra is only close to male genitals. One thought is that for the first two chakras the glands are reversed for males and females. The second chakra is closer to the ovaries.

In crystal healing, the Base Chakra can be used to bring energy down from the higher centres and to assist in grounding people. That is to link the earth to the Base Chakra and to link the higher energy chakras to the Base Chakra, thereby providing a balanced energy flow. The chakra links into the body's nervous system. The Base Chakra is at the base of the spine and through the spine come a very large number of nerves. If we consider the spine to be a tree then the Base Chakra is at the bottom of the tree trunk from which the root system emerges. The Base Chakra is at the bottom of the other chakras; it is the foundation stone for the other six major chakras to grow from.

On the physical plane the Base Chakra relates to the grounding and base structure of the body, the parts that support us – the feet and legs and the bones. It also relates to the large intestine, which extracts fluid and some nutrients from our food and removes all remaining rubbish, thus helping us to survive. The element that relates to the Base Chakra is earth, providing a solid basis and support for survival. At a basic level, the earth provides our survival needs; it is what we are most closely connected to on a daily basis. We use statements such as feeling grounded, which relate to using the earth energies as a support and enabling us to deal with crisis and therefore survive. The vibrational rate of the Base Chakra is the slowest of the major seven chakras, the vibration that is nearest solid matter.

The Base Chakra is often one of the easiest to identify as being out of balance. In some ways it is a sign of the times that so many Base Chakras are out of balance. Many people suffer from stress, or spend a lot of time in their heads for reasons of work or just life in general. Both of these situations are potentially damaging to the Base Chakra. Stress overuses the adrenal gland so that it either shuts down through overuse or is running all the time pushing more adrenalin into the body, which overexerts it. At the same time the Base Chakra, directly linked to the adrenal gland, also suffers and may well shut down or disconnect from its source of energy, the earth. In pre-stress society, stress still existed but normally with breaks in between stressful times; it was short-lived stress. Today there is rarely any break from stress, even that great relaxing device in the corner, the television, can create stress both by the emission from the electronics and from the programming which is designed to keep our attention. The modern world pays great attention to intellect, often to the disadvantage of the physical side of life. In this case, the Base Chakra is forgotten, as the person concentrates on the higher chakras. In a perfect world, the influences on the individual would be redressed and the chakras would all be in balance. In a similar way, other people escape from the real world by living in an artificial world in their heads.

Chakra 2

The second chakra is called the Sacral Chakra from its position near the sacrum on the spine. There is occasionally confusion with the term Navel Chakra. The Sacral Chakra resides just below the navel although the Navel Chakra is sometimes shown above the navel; it, of course, varies from person to person. The only way to find the position of a chakra is by using a pendulum or your hand. This will be dealt with later. The Sacral Chakra has a vibrational rate that is slightly higher than the Base Chakra, because, as the energy moves up through the chakras, it becomes more refined from the earth plane through to the spiritual plane. Unlike the Base Chakra, the Sacral Chakra has a connection into the body at the front and at the rear. When you scan the chakras, you can feel chakras 2 to 6 at the front and at the back of the body, chakra 1 and chakra 7 are a pair in their own right.

The second chakra is often referred to as the chakra that relates to creativity. This creativity probably relates to procreation as well as the creativity associated with developing new ideas. The chakra is related to the testes and ovaries, or following the arguments for the Base Chakra, the ovaries and the adrenal gland, for women and men respectively. This makes sense in many ways: if you can survive – the purpose of Chakra 1 – you will want your species to continue, so you procreate – the purpose of Chakra 2. That is for women; for men it may be to procreate and then to survive. Within the human race, the act of procreation has also led to sexuality and pleasure. A balanced second chakra can also provide an individual with self-confidence and vitality.

The Sacral Chakra is closely linked to water. As the first chakra relates to the earth, the second chakra relates to the moon. The moon in many philosophies connects to liquids or fluidity and emotions. As well as the testes and ovaries, the second chakra is associated with the womb, kidneys, circulation system and the bladder – the parts of the body that deal with fluids and the large and small intestines which assist in removing water from our waste products. When the Second Chakra is out of balance there may be problems in one or more of these areas. The second chakra is also linked to the sixth chakra and to the astral component of the individual. A well-balanced and open second chakra can assist in psychic skills.

The qualities of the second chakra tend to be childlike; they are creative, innocent and trusting. Even the position of the chakra is where the embryo grows which is a direct link to creativity, water – the womb, and the innocence of the child.

The normal colour for the second chakra is orange, a very vibrant, energetic and creative colour. Lighter and more outward looking than red, orange can assist in the creative process with a cheerful and exciting energy.

Chakra 3

More commonly known as the Solar Plexus Chakra, this is positioned just below the sternum in the area which, if you are hit there, knocks the wind out of you. The colour is yellow, like its namesake the sun. This is the chakra of will and power, together with self-worth and where you fit within the cosmic all. The Solar Plexus Chakra is where, at times of stress, you may feel butterflies. In addition, at times of crisis the feeling may be as if someone has physically knocked the wind out of you. Together with the adrenal gland, the solar plexus is the major area that is affected by stress and tension. The chakra relates to intense emotion represented by anger, laughter and joy.

The third chakra is connected to many of the major organs within the body. The associated gland is the pancreas, and linked body parts include liver, gall bladder, spleen, stomach, diaphragm and digestive system. These organs are related to our emotions and tensions. The gall bladder is associated with bitterness – in both senses as the bile it produces is very bitter and a person who is bitter often has associated gall bladder problems. The liver is related to anger and jealousy, there are butterflies in the stomach from fear, which can also affect the digestive system. The digestive system transforms solid and liquid food into energy. The third chakra has the element of fire and uses the two lower chakras, earth and water, along with air form the fourth chakra to create energy by 'burning' food. Like fire, the body needs air for effective metabolism of food and energy.

The Solar Plexus Chakra is an adult chakra although much of its training came from our parents. The early years set the scene for the ability of the individual to put forward their will and to take responsibility for their own power. Because of this, there can be serious conflict between the second and third chakra with their creativity and personal will. Parents and society, whose messages are taken in by the third chakra, may well remove the natural exuberance of the child. Within the world, there are changes in the structures that relate to power, which filter down through levels of society. Many people are now saying that they are regaining their own power, whereas not so long ago they would have been suppressed and accepted their lot. This is not an easy process to undertake and the change in individuals' will and power can lead to changes in the way society reacts to the individual. Unfortunately, this occasionally sets up conflict with those who have yet to accept their own power and are working on the rules laid down by others as to how they should utilise their own power. This sounds like a call to anarchy but is rather a call to the individual to recognise that they have their own power and the right to assert it for their own self-worth.

When the third chakra is out of balance there may be symptoms such as diabetes or eating disorders and ulcers. When properly balanced, the individual is in a better state to deal with fear, able to direct their energies towards their aims and complete them, to have patience and internal strength to deal with problems, to know who they are and use their emotions in a positive energetic way.

The energy of the third chakra is fire and the planet representation is the sun. The essences of the energies are becoming more rarefied and volatile as we work up through the chakras. The energy of fire is burning and rising with the heat. Just as fire transforms solid materials into heat and light, the internal element of fire can also flare up. This can relate to the dramatic emotional part of the chakra with laughter or anger, both of which, having been contained, can flare up. The third chakra takes the solidness of the earth and the flowing action of the water and transforms the energies of the first two chakras into action.

Chakra 4

This is the middle chakra and thought to join the bottom three physical chakras with the top three spiritual chakras. The fourth chakra is known as the Heart Chakra and is positioned about three or four fingers' width up from the bottom of the sternum. There seems to be an indentation in the bone at the Heart Chakra. The model that is being used here considers that the chakras are all in a vertical line. This appears to work, but it is possible that they are not in a straight line and are placed over parts of the body that are more relevant to their names. If you cannot find a particular chakra, therefore, try moving around the area and you may find that it is in a slightly different position. In addition, as each person is structured differently, with varying proportions, natural rhythms and energies, it would seem that their chakras could also be in different places. When looking for the Heart Chakra do not go too far towards the throat as there is another strong chakra, the Thymus Chakra, lying just above the Heart Chakra.

The Heart Chakra relates to the thymus gland, even though there is a separate chakra at that point. Other related body parts include the lungs, heart, arms and shoulders. The element that relates to the Heart Chakra is air, which links into the lungs. This is also the link to the third chakra to provide air for the burning of solid matter to release energy, and to the fifth chakra, which uses the air for communication via the voice. These links are why it is important for the chakras to be in balance and for the subtle energy connections between them to be in good order. The fourth chakra relates to love; this is the selfless Universal Love as well as the personal love between individuals. Like the third chakra, the values and views of love are often instilled in the childhood years. The unselfish Universal Love that can also be seen as compassion is often put aside, particularly by western society. So it may involve a lot of work to bring this chakra back to its full glory.

When fully opened to Universal Love the person may notice an increase in their compassion, a better ability to feel both solid and energetic forces, an increase in their sensitivity to the needs of others. If the third chakra is also balanced then this will work well, if not they may give their power to other people in what they consider as love; real love is a healthy balance not subservience. They will also be free to give and, just as important, to receive. When the fourth chakra is out of balance, the physical symptoms may include lung-related diseases such as asthma and problems associated to the heart and blood pressure. The tales of people suffering from a broken heart may well relate to the damage done to the Heart Chakra by moving away from the concept of Universal Love and oneness.

In some ways, the Heart Chakra is very difficult to work within modern society. What it requires may not be easily available. Acceptance of Universal Love does not seem to be recognised, leaving love to be generated between two individuals. This in turn puts demands on those individuals, which is not in the best interests of love or the relationship. In addition, the real spiritual side of life seems, in many cases, to be in decline. This lack of spirituality is placing a restriction on people's view of the greater dimension of where we fit into the world and universe. This realm of compassion and Universal Love is being denied to people by their own actions. As such, this links with the third chakra in terms of where people fit into the larger picture, which in turn either puts them in a lost situation or brings out their ego and selfishness in greater amounts causing imbalance, pain and loss.

Because of the position of the Heart Chakra, and because of the way we live, it is often out of balance from a very early age. The colour of the Heart Chakra is normally given as green, as this fits in with the seven rainbow colour model, or, because it is the colour of love, pink. Pink suffers as it is commonly attributed to girls causing even greater problems in people accepting it as a loving colour. The heart can appear to have many colours from gold through to very dark and cold colours.

Chakra 5

Having dealt with the basic physical chakras and the linking Heart Chakra, we now move into the more ethereal chakras, the first of which is the Throat Chakra. Traditionally it is positioned on the front of the body at the soft indentation at the top of the sternum. This is a sensitive place most of the time but even more so for those with an imbalanced Throat Chakra. The glands associated with this chakra are the thyroid and parathyroid, which are positioned very close to each other in the neck. Not surprisingly one aspect of the Throat Chakra is communication of all sorts. The voice can transmit our needs, feelings, emotions and our thoughts and ideas. Even the youngest of babies has a voice to attract attention to get their needs met and to communicate their pleasure and love.

Unfortunately, as we grow, we are conditioned to what we can say and when we can say it. This tends to reduce our ability to communicate the real factors that are essential for our well-being. For instance, boys are taught not to cry when upset, so the sobbing that comes from deep within us cannot be expressed through the throat. This form of conditioning stays with us into adult life, when in the western world at least, we tend to find communication about ourselves very difficult. The fifth chakra is the communication device for all the other chakras. To help understand this, imagine a flow of energy from the root chakra moving upwards. As it passes the other chakras, it collects more information at higher vibrational rates until it reaches the Throat Chakra where it has the opportunity to be expressed. However, if the Throat Chakra is out of balance or as it is sometimes referred to, blocked, then this flow of information is also blocked and it is held within the body. It may be expressed in different ways, which are not good for the overall health of the individual, possibly bursting out physically, emotionally or mentally.

The body parts that are associated with this chakra are the neck and shoulders, a very common place for holding tension and stress, and the arms and hands. When the chakra is out of balance physical symptoms can include problems with the related glands with an under- or overactive thyroid, stiff neck and frozen shoulder, sore throats and possibly associated colds which seem to lie on the upper chest. There may also be problems with speech, including poor self-expression, not stopping talking and speech impediments.

This chakra is also linked to creativity, also associated to the second chakra. The Throat Chakra, the chakra of communication, enables the creativity to be expressed. This manifestation need not only be by voice as the chakra also relates to the arms and hands, so that the expression of creativity can be through another medium such as drawing or writing. There may also be an increase in the ability to connect with the greater consciousness of the universe, where much of creativity can be drawn from. Of course, creativity may come from the greater consciousness that resides within oneself, but the result will be the same. Within our language, we have sayings such as 'the idea came out of thin air' and many of the most creative people through the ages have implied that their ideas came to them from 'out there', either in dreams or just appeared in their heads. This ties in with another property of this chakra, the element associated with it, which is given a variety of names such as ether, spirit or sound. It is the fifth element after earth, water, fire and air, and is the ethereal, the non-physical element that is part of every person.

Chakra 6

The sixth chakra, the Brow Chakra, which in earlier texts is called the third eye, is positioned in the centre of the brow about two fingers' width above the bridge of the nose. This chakra deals with perception, intuition and seeing in all senses of the word. It is associated to the pineal gland and the eyes. The sixth chakra is to do with the psychic power of the individual. The problem is that, within our culture, many people are forced either to close their third eye or not talk about it. This is slowly changing with even governments admitting that they have experimented with using people as perceivers and distant viewers.

A blocked or imbalanced Brow Chakra may lead to headaches, problems with sight and difficulties sleeping and dreams including nightmares. With a balanced sixth chakra, and if all the chakras are also balanced, the awareness and perception of the individual can be very dramatic. Not everyone has the same abilities; the perceptive abilities can be pictorial, audio, or a combination of both. There is also the ability to just know. Many people know who is on the telephone. Many mothers have known when one of their children is in danger. Some people instinctively seem to know when things are going to happen to them. They may get a message, they may 'see' the event, or they may have a dream. All of these activities can be enhanced if the Brow Chakra is allowed to open.

The colour associated with the Brow Chakra is indigo, mainly because it is the sixth colour of the rainbow. The colour can be almost anything depending on what is happening to the individual. Furthermore, there is no element associated to this chakra, since its energies are beyond the realms of the physical, and beyond those of the ether associated with the Throat Chakra. There is a link to the Sacral Chakra.

Chakra 7

This is the last of the major seven chakras. This chakra, the Crown Chakra, is the one that makes the connection to everything else. Whatever your spiritual beliefs, this chakra assists in making your true connection to your spiritual being, a connection with everything, everybody, every being and event in the cosmos. In modern society, very few people have a fully developed seventh chakra. Those, who for some reason have had their Crown Chakra opened, can find it a very disturbing event. They may see pictures of events that are taking place elsewhere or they may be in a strange world or in fact anywhere in the universe. The realms of the Crown Chakra do not follow the normal rules we associate with time, space and perception.

The Crown Chakra is situated at the top of the head, it is associated with the pituitary gland, the cerebral cortex, the central nervous system and through this to the whole body. The colour given to it from the rainbow set is violet, but it is all colours, as it associates with all things.

When it is out of balance or blocked the person may feel alienated and confused at many levels, from their personal life through to their connection, or lack of connection, to their spiritual beliefs. Their behaviour may be that of a depressed person and they may find learning difficult, leading to yet deeper depression. However, once the Crown Chakra is opened and if all the other chakras are balanced the person will reach an amazing state of well-being and become very aware, open and blissed out. This is possibly what happened to all the great religious leaders and prophets, that they opened and balanced all their chakras.

The Auras

The last few pages have given a very broad overview of the chakras. They are used in crystal healing for diagnosis and for healing. Another part of the subtle energy system of importance to us is the auras. These are layers that surround the body. Each layer serves a different purpose and each layer appears to become more rarefied as it gets further away from the body. The exact number of auric layers is not known; different people seem to consider different numbers of layers. Another unknown is whether each layer is only at the level of the layer, like an onion or whether it

Figure 4.2   The auric layers

reaches to the body from its outer level, so that each auric layer is represented close to the body and at the furthest layer only one layer exists. This last image, perhaps, provides the best way of understanding what the aura is and how it works.

All the layers of the aura near the body form a dense region of subtle energy that is closer in energetic value to the physical body than the individual layers furthest from the body. Each layer has a certain energy that can stretch a given distance from the body; the higher the frequency of the energy the further out it can reach. The idea is that the higher the frequency the less the influence of the physical body has in restricting the expansion of the energy field (see Figure 4.2).

The names given to each layer seem to vary with every person who writes or talks on the subject. Although this can be confusing the important factor is to understand what each layer is, the chakra it is related to and how to work with them. Many people have had an experience similar to the following. You are standing in a room, possibly with lots of other people. You have your back to the door as it opens and a person enters the room, yet you know who it is before you turn around. Why or how? The answer is that the aura of the other person and your aura connected before your vision recognised the other person. You recognised the pattern of the other person, or your auras exchanged data, which were sent back to your subtle body, which linked to your mind so that you sensed the other person. This form of action tends to happen with those that you know well, as you have spent time in each other's auric fields and have a stronger connection or recognition. It can also happen with those people that you have experienced fear with, such as an unknown person in an accident.

Etheric layer

The aura, like the rest of the subtle energy we are looking at, is of a very high frequency and the frequency becomes higher the further from the body the field reaches. The field nearest the body has a lower frequency. This field is the etheric layer. It acts like a pattern for the actual physical body to grow into. Again, there are still differing views on how this happens. One view considers the etheric layer to be a blueprint the physical components of the body follow as they grow; sometimes they do not follow the pattern correctly. The other view is that the etheric layer is a mould into which the body grows. When it reaches the size of the mould it stops growing.

This aura is strongly associated with the first chakra, the Base Chakra. Both are to do with the physical body, the basis of life and survival. However, the chakra is also connected to all of the other auric layers, each of which is directly linked to a separate chakra. This means that all of the chakras are interconnected through the different auric layers as well as the body. This is why crystal healing is part of the school of holistic medicine. If one chakra or auric layer is looked at in isolation, information from other areas is included in that chakra but not the whole story, so that all the chakras need to be checked and all the layers need to be analysed. It does mean that by analysing the chakras, an idea about the auras can be developed and then they can be looked at. This close association is useful as the auras are harder to work with than the chakras.

Emotional layer

The second auric layer is the emotional layer. This, as its name implies, relates to the feelings of the individual. If there are difficulties with emotions, this second layer may feel thick or 'soupy' so that it is difficult to move your hand through it. This is one way to check and analyse chakras. Using a sweeping motion at different heights above the body it is possible to feel any areas that are out of balance. Checking the chakras and the auras can be like trying to recreate the person and their problems in the form of a three-dimensional model. When scanning over the body you may also pick up feelings from physical problems within the body, which have misshapen the aura, or where the misshapen aura has created physical difficulties. If the physical problem is caused by emotional difficulties then the emotional layer will also be distorted. This is where the questions at the beginning of a session help by providing a framework on to which to put the scanning of the chakras and auras.

Mental layer

The next layer outwards from the body is the mental layer. This is an important area. The saying 'that every action starts with a thought' can be seen operating here. The information from the mental layer filters down through the emotional layer to the physical layer where it can take form. The idea of mind over matter, particularly when considering the health of an individual, can also be appreciated using this model. The mental layer relates to the third chakra, which is to do with the self and the person's personal power. Again, the mental aspect enables the individual to take their own power and create their personal will.

Astral layer

The fourth layer is the astral layer. This, like the Heart Chakra, is the link between the physical auras and the more ethereal and spiritual layers. It may act as a transforming layer taking the very high frequency energies of the higher levels and changing them so that they can be used at the mental, emotional and physical levels. The energies of the astral level may be those that interconnect with other energies during dreaming. The term astral travel is used for the experience where the person seems to go to different realms when sleeping or in trance-like states and it may be that the frequency of the astral layer is one that can connect to other energies providing the feeling of being elsewhere.

Spiritual layer

After the fourth layer the information about the auric layers becomes less clear. Different people see or feel different things. It is probably best to say that beyond the astral layer there is at least one more layer, which can be termed the spiritual layer. This layer could be considered part of our soul. These higher layers may provide information for the lower layers from a greater source of energy. It is at these levels that a form of psychic connection between people can take place. The spiritual layers may extend beyond the body by a considerable distance. It is not uncommon for people to 'feel' another person is close by, perhaps in another room or even in the same town. At times of extreme energy changes, such as danger or pain it appears that some people know that another person, normally someone close to them is in danger even if they are thousands of miles away. Part of this may be links via the higher levels of the aura and, as some people express it, we are all one. Because of the interlinking of the chakras and the aura, there may also be strong connections through the chakras. In particular with those who are very close, such as mother and child or those that are in love. The strongest of these may come from the Heart Chakra, but all the chakras will interreact with those of the other person creating, hopefully, two-way links.

Where the links are one way, one person is putting out feelings towards another, who, for whatever reason, does not reciprocate there can be a build-up of imbalanced energy and a possible drain on the person who is not reciprocating.

Finally, there is a lot written about the distances of each auric layer from the body, from a quarter of an inch to tens of feet. There is, of course, a difference in these measurements between everybody. The only way to find out is to test them for each person to see where you perceive them to be. There is an exercise to do this at the end of this unit.

EXERCISES

This unit has dealt with two key components in the subtle energy fields found in all of us and the exercises are about learning to find and understand these energies.

The first one is to try to find your own chakras. Prepare a quiet space where you will not be disturbed. Preferably somewhere where you can lie down or move around. You may also find it easier if you are dressed in loose, light clothing. Keep your journal nearby and write down your results as you work on each chakra. Make sure you date each piece of work, as it can be helpful to see when certain feelings were found and what was happening to you at the time. The chakras can normally be found physically and energetically (see Figure 4.1). First try the physical approach: Make yourself comfortable and as relaxed as possible. Set the scene with gentle lighting and make sure the environment is warm enough. If you are cold then you will find it harder to relax. The first chakra is between the anus and the genitals; normally there is an indentation and it may feel tender or as if your fingers will sink into it forever. Sit, squat or kneel so you can easily position your hand in this area. Gently explore the area about halfway between your genitals and your anus along a centre line between the two. You should find a small indentation. Massage this area gently with your fingers to help stimulate it. Then place the palm of your hand over the area and very slowly move it so that it is about two inches away from your body. The centre of the palm is your sensor; you may have to try both hands to see which is the more sensitive. You may feel the energy that is generated by this chakra.

What do you feel? If you do not feel anything do not worry, carry on with the exercise. Some people feel warmth or cold, others feel a tingling sensation or a pulse. Some people get information or a picture. There is no correct feeling or sensation. The important thing is to keep your mind as clear as possible, remain relaxed and trust any sensations you perceive.

When working on other people it is a good idea not to place your hand in this personal area. Instead, if the client is lying down use your hand over the front of the area without touching, as if you were smoothing the area (see Figure 4.3).

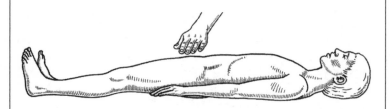

Figure 4.3   Locating the chakras

Next we move on to the Sacral Chakra. Physically, this is the hardest to find. It is approximately two fingers' width down from the navel. If you gently walk your fingers down from the navel, feel for a sensation of your hand sinking, or for an indentation. If you do not find anything, do not worry. You may find it easier to sense for this chakra. Rub your hands together, then using the palm of your hand place it so that the centre of the palm is roughly in the appropriate area. Place your hand on your body and very gently lift it upwards until you are approximately two inches above your body. Sometimes moving the hand backwards and forwards or in a circular movement increases the ability to feel the chakras. So try moving your hand up and down the body and away from the body and back again. Again, what do you feel?

Onwards and upwards to discover the Solar Plexus Chakra. This is reasonably easy to locate. Find the sternum or the breastbone. Place your first finger on the bottom of this bone and press in with your second finger (see Figure 4.4). When you gently press in there may be a slight pain or a feeling of being knocked in the

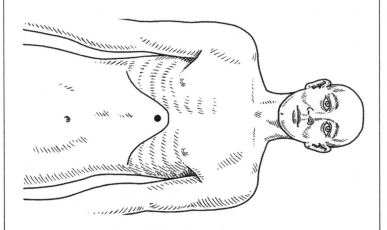

Figure 4.4   The Solar Plexus Chakra

stomach with a slight nauseous sensation. Again, feel above this area with your open hand. Write down your results.

Next is the Heart Chakra. This is located on the sternum about one third of the way up between the breasts; physically there is an indentation in the bone which can be found with your fingertips. Place your hand over the area to see what sensations you can perceive. On to the Throat Chakra, which is positioned just above the collarbone on the centre line of the body. There is an indentation that when pressed may cause feelings of nausea. Then try to feel the energy of the chakra with your hand. If you do not perceive any sensations try moving your hand in small circles and then moving away from and then back towards the body.

The last two major chakras are the brow and the crown. Neither of these has a physical presence that is easy to find. The Brow Chakra is about one finger width above the eyebrows on the centre line of the body. When it is very active, there may be a tight feeling across the forehead. Try feeling for the energy by moving your hand in and out of the area as this chakra works at very high frequencies. The Crown Chakra is on top of the head and can be very sensitive. Some people do not like having the top of their head touched for that reason. Feel from the front to the back of the head until you find a sensitive spot, then try holding your hand over that place and note what you feel.

Finally to the feet. Hold one foot so that the palm of your hand is parallel with the sole of the foot and about two inches away. Move your hand around and note what you find. Repeat on the other foot. The feet chakras are an important part of our grounding process. Look at your notes to see if your readings make any sense when related to what is going on in your life at the moment or to how you feel.

The next part of this exercise is to repeat the process on someone else. This time you will not be touching them, just trying to feel their chakras when your hand is away from the body. The best approach is in a quiet, warm room where there will be no distractions. If possible, have your client lie down on their back.

Start at the Base Chakra and work your way up, returning to the feet at the end. You may also like to do the same at the knees and over the hands. At this stage do not worry about interpretation, just concentrate on finding the chakras.

The next exercise also requires a person, again lying down. This time start a long way out from the person with both palms facing them. Move slowly towards them noting any sensations or areas that are hard to push against. Work from the side so that you are feeling the auras rather than the chakras. As you get closer, you may find several layers. Try to feel through your hands what they represent, you can also try to visualise them.

An alternative method that you can use for finding both chakras and auric layers is by using your trusted pendulum. This can be achieved in two ways, either by using the pendulum directly or by using the pendulum as an indicator for the other hand, which is undertaking the feeling. Whichever way you choose, place the hand/pendulum over the body so that it is about two to three inches away and move it to the approximate position asking if this is the (named) chakra, keep moving in little steps giving the pendulum time to reestablish itself. For aura hunting, using the pendulum in one hand and feeling with the other is possibly best. This means that you may be able to sense the auric layer with your hand at the same time. You can also ask relevant questions including if this is a particular layer. This exercise will give you an idea as to how far out the auric layers are.

Try these exercises several times to familiarise yourself with the positioning and responses of the major chakras and auric layers.

UNIT 5 – BASIC CRYSTAL HEALING

This is where you start working with the crystals you have obtained, cleansed and energised. This unit will deal with the use of Clear Quartz. From this basis, the rest of your crystal work will grow. There are four sections to the treatment: the first is for you; the second is to find out about the person you are working with; the third is the treatment; and lastly, to ensure that the client is safe to enter back into the real world. All of these stages are important and care should be taken at each one. Please remember that these are guidelines on how to work, not rules set in stone. If you find other ways or read of other ways that seem better for the way you work then as long as they do not endanger the client or yourself use them.

Preparation

The first phase is the preparation of yourself and your working space. If you and your working space are not prepared, the client may not feel safe and confident and any healing will be hampered. So, cleanse your working space physically and psychically with smudge or essential oils. Make sure your crystals are ready and have been cleansed and charged since their last use or if they have been left for a long period. Refer back to the previous units for assistance. Make sure the lighting is not too bright or subdued. If you get direct sunlight that will shine on the client draw the curtains to help them feel comfortable; as much as the sun is healing, in this situation it can make people feel uncomfortable with its heat or light.

Now prepare yourself. Before your client arrives, allow yourself half an hour to meditate and make contact with your guides. You may also find it helpful to undertake a grounding exercise in the time so that you are feeling solid and confident in your work. The first few times you work with crystals, you may well feel nervous and wonder if what you are doing is correct. When this happens make sure you contact your guide and that you are grounded. If necessary quickly send roots from your feet into the ground and connect with the orange golden light that is the grounding energy. Set your intent for the session in a form similar to this: 'My work with [name of client] is for the higher good, with the intention of assisting them help themselves.'

Finally, very simple things such as switch off the telephone and put a note on the door (after the client arrives) asking not to be disturbed. Go to the toilet as it is not good practise to leave the person on their own and it is very hard to concentrate when your bladder is sending urgent messages.

Starting the treatment

When your client arrives (they may be a member of the household who has come from the kitchen, but the method remains exactly the same), welcome them, take their coat and, if you are not wearing shoes in your workroom, ask them to remove their shoes before entering. When they come into the room ask them to sit down and make sure they are comfortable. As you do this look at them carefully. A lot can be gained about each person from their skin colour and texture, the way they stand and sit as well as body posture and how they react. Make notes as you go along. Try to talk with them as you do this, as it is not an interrogation. Next, use a questionnaire to obtain more information. This has been dealt with in Unit 2. Write down their responses as you go, but keep your attention focused on them. If necessary just note important words, you can always add to it later when you have more time.

This is, of course, the time to find out about any contra-indications. Although crystal healing is very safe, there are times, especially at the beginning of your work when it is best not to work on people with specific conditions. These are dealt with in detail in Unit 2. However, if the person is pregnant, has severe heart problems, epilepsy or diabetes then suggest, in the nicest possible way, that they see someone more experienced. There may be other conditions that you do not feel like dealing with including cancer and AIDS. As a healer, you have the right to say no. You do not have to treat everyone who comes knocking at your door, only those you want to. You can always say no, you do not have to give a reason and you must not give in to a persistent caller. Again, this is a situation where you must listen to the inner voice of your intuition and respond in the appropriate manner.

Deciding where to work

Having looked at the person and taken a case history you should have some idea why they have come to see you (apart from the fact you asked them to be a case study!). Take a minute or so to bring this information together: are there any areas that are not clear, if so ask some questions to clear up any possible doubt or misunderstanding you may have. When people come for treatments, they often forget important aspects. This is probably because they are nervous of you, or the environment and the treatment may well appear strange to them. In addition, it is rare that anyone has the opportunity to express opinions about themselves in a non-judgemental situation. It is with an empathetic (not sympathetic) ear that you listen to your clients. A gentle nod, or even repeating what they have said so that they can hear that you have understood them will help them relax and provide more information.

Now ask your client to take up the position you want them in to begin work, and make sure they are comfortable. Small cushions under the base of the back and behind the knees can reduce tension in the back muscles caused by lying down. Ask them to relax as much as they can. Suggest that they take in a deep breath and blow it out. Most people will do this but very quietly and politely. What you want is for them really to expel the air, quickly and noisily, so that they also expel the daily tension that has built up inside them. Get them to repeat this three times. If they have not already done so suggest that they close their eyes.

Scanning

Then explain that you are going to pass your hand over them and use a pendulum. As you are doing this work as quietly and gently as possible. If you can get all the way around the person then start on one side at the heart area and gently introduce your hand into their close aura. Remember to approach them very carefully, because even though at this proximity you are already in their aura, sudden actions and movements towards their more physical auras may be uncomfortable for them. Slowly move your hand from side to side covering more and more of the body nearest to you. Note any areas that feel different, warmer, colder or tingly in some way. Relate what you find to your previous information but do not prejudge the situation. If you have been told that there is a problem with a particular part of the body, do not make yourself perceive something that is not there.

Cover the whole of the body from the centre line towards you, including the side and the arms. Move up to the head and then down the leg. Now move to the other side of the person and repeat using the same hand. It does not matter if you repeat areas, in fact it can be useful as you may become more sensitised as you work. When you have finished note down any findings on a chart. A diagram of a body is very useful to mark places of interest on.

Do the same thing again but this time with a pendulum. There are two basic ways of using the pendulum for this work. The first is the direct method with the pendulum over the body and the second is to hold the pendulum in one hand while scanning over the body with the other hand. Which you use is up to you, but do try both methods several times. You can try both methods on the same person in the same session to see if you get similar results. The crucial thing in both cases is to ask the correct questions. What do you want the pendulum to tell you? Normally the question should relate to whether there are any areas to work on with crystals. If there was an area you found when scanning you can use the pendulum to ask questions about the area and even how to use crystals on it. You can ask about the area's connection to a particular chakra (see the Unit 6).

An important area to start practising in is feeling the energy in the aura. When you first approach the person try to feel any layers and what they feel like. When you are scanning with your hand and pendulum, move your hand up and down to get an impression of the auric layers. If you stay within 18 inches of the body you will probably come across only three layers, with two of these being fairly close to the body. You may find that your hand feels as if it is skimming along the surface of something, rather like skimming a stone across the surface of a pond. If you get this, try to move through the area to see what it feels like further in. Sometimes it feels as if it is not possible. The client may have a block that prevents people from getting too close or it may be the result of some form of trauma. Depending where this strong or thick layer is you may get an indication as to whether it is related to the physical, emotional, mental or spiritual part of the person.

Using the crystal

However, keep things simple for this first session. By now, you should have a clear idea of any areas that need working upon. If you have not found any then you can still give a simple balancing treatment as described in this section. You will need your Clear Quartz point for this work.

Place the crystal in your receiving hand (see Unit 3), with the point up towards your wrist, over the area you want to work on (see Figure 5.1). Point your other hand to the floor away from the client. Then with the intention of removing negative energy and sending it to the earth for transmutation to positive energy, circle the hand with the crystal in an anti-clockwise manner. Keep your movements slow and small. After a minute or so, you may feel a change in your moving hand. If not use your intuition to assess when you have removed the negative energy. Depending on the nature of the problem one treatment may not be enough; it may take several to complete the work. For chronic situations, it is possible that no treatment will reverse the problem, only slow down any worsening of the symptoms.

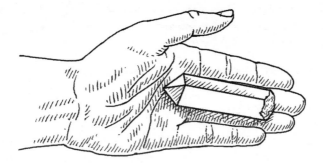

Figure 5.1   Receiving hand

Charging the chakra

Now place the crystal in your other hand, the sending hand, with the point towards your fingers (see Figure 5.2), and hold your receiving hand palm up. Imagine a flow of positive energy passing from the universe into your hand, up your arm, across your neck, down your other arm, into the crystal and into your client. Move the hand holding the crystal in a clockwise motion over the area of concern. Using your intuition and how your hand feels assess when you have worked enough. Sometimes moving the crystal becomes harder or easier. If it becomes easier when removing energy it implies that the task is complete and that the negative energy has been removed. If it becomes harder when applying positive energy,

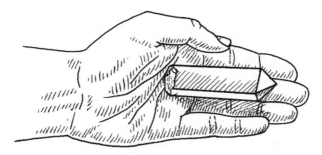

Figure 5.2   Sending hand

it indicates that the area is becoming full. With the first treatment and when you are not sure always take the cautious route by giving shorter rather than longer treatments.

Simple Clear Quartz balancing treatment

A simple balancing treatment can be applied as well or if there are no symptoms instead of the previous treatment. This uses the same technique on each of the chakras. Chakras by their nature are rarely in balance or perfect harmony. The idea of this balance treatment is to assist the chakras regain their balance and accord. Be very careful when working on the chakras, as they are important subtle energy communication points and although they often need external assistance, they remain very sensitive to subtle energy sources including crystals.

Your client should still be lying on their back. Do not let them lie for more than 30 minutes unless necessary, as they will begin to get uncomfortable. This balance starts with the Base Chakra and because of its position we work to the front of the chakra, above the area of the pubic bone, not touching the body. Take your Clear Quartz crystal in your receiving hand with the point towards your wrist, position it just above the front of the Base Chakra and point your other hand towards the earth, away from your client. Gently rotate your receiving hand in an anti-clockwise direction, moving it away from the client's body. As you do this, visualise any negative energy being removed and sent to the earth through your hand. If you feel inclined, repeat this several times. Then reverse your hands so that the crystal is in your sending hand with the point towards your fingers and your receiving hand is palm up.

Energising the chakra

Rotate the hand with the crystal in a clockwise manner above the chakra while visualising universal healing energy coming through your hand and going across into the crystal and being amplified and sent into the chakra. You can start away from the body and as you rotate the crystal in a clockwise direction, move in towards the body, that is, in a spiralling movement. It is important when working like this to ensure that all the negative energy is sent to the earth and not held by you. However, with the positive energy coming from the universe it can be useful if you receive some of that as it passes through your arms and neck.

Now move up to the Sacral Chakra and repeat the same two processes. At any time during this balancing the client may make some comment or react in some other way. If they do, remain grounded, do not panic, stay with what you are doing. Talk to them and if necessary reassure them that they are all right. When you have finished the Sacral Chakra, go the Solar Plexus Chakra and again repeat the two processes. Then onto the Heart Chakra, Throat Chakra, Brow Chakra and finally the Crown Chakra. When you have finished let the client be still for as long as possible, upwards of 15 minutes. When they are ready help them into a sitting position and see what they have to say. You can ask them how they feel or whether they noticed any effects, changes or feelings.

Check the client

If they seem as if they are not really with it or grounded, get them to move and think of physical things such as birds, meals, flowers, anything that relates to the physical world. Suggest that they do not drive for a while and that, if possible, they have a hot drink and a snack to eat – something simple like dried fruit can be effective.

Working in the auric layers

When you were scanning the client, you may have noticed different feelings at different levels, which implies different auric layers. These can be worked on using your Clear Quartz crystal. It depends what the feelings were. If there appeared to be a thick layer that was difficult to move through, then you may feel that this needs to be removed. To do this, hold your Clear Quartz so that you can sweep through this layer using the side of the crystal. Move the crystal in a horizontal manner sweeping the thick layer to the earth (see Figure 5.3). Start at the head and move down through the body. As you reach the end of the sweep, shake or flick the crystal asking this negative energy to be sent to the earth and transmuted into positive energy. Repeat the sweeping movement from head to toes. After this, you can work from the body's centre line outwards in shorter sweeps. When you have done this, check how the layer feels and whether it may need an input to replace the negative energy.

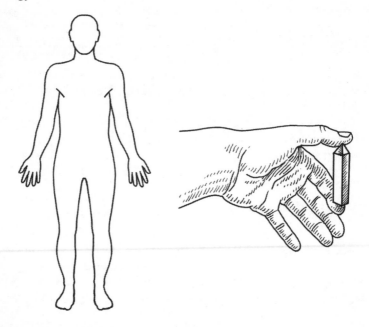

Figure 5.3   Sweeping the auric layer

To replace the negative energy with positive energy hold the crystal in your sending hand in the same way so that you can sweep through the aura. Hold your receiving hand palm up and ask for healing energy to be given to this part of the aura and repeat the sweeping process. Again check the aura by scanning with your hand or pendulum and see how it feels. Sometimes it may take several sessions to complete the work. In addition, the area may feel weak or vulnerable for a while and the client may have similar feelings. This is because the part that has been removed has been taking energy from the whole area and the surroundings and it takes a while for the system to return to a healthy balance. There will be more work on the aura in the next unit.

Two clear quartz crystals

All of the work in this unit so far has used a single Clear Quartz crystal. Now we will work with two Clear Quartz crystals. This is not necessarily better than one crystal, it may give a more specific result for some things, but it is not always twice as powerful. The way to use two crystals is with one crystal in each hand. In your receiving hand place the crystal with the point towards your wrist and in your sending hand the point is towards your fingers. When you want to remove energy from a person, hold the receiving hand over the area under consideration and with the sending hand and its crystal pointing towards the earth circle the hand in an anti-clockwise direction. To place positive healing energy into an area hold the receiving hand palm up and circle the sending hand in a clockwise direction over the area to be worked on.

Clearing and replacing energy

To work on a specific area or a chakra with two crystals, the stages before using the crystals remain the same. To clear the area hold one crystal in your receiving hand with the point towards your wrist over the area you wish to work on. In your sending hand, place the crystal so that the point is towards your fingers and your fingers are pointing towards the ground. Move your sending hand in an anti-clockwise circular movement. As the clearing is completed, you may feel that your sending hand moves more easily. To replace the removed energy, place your sending hand with the crystal still pointing towards the fingertips over the area and hold your receiving hand palm up with the crystal still pointing towards your wrist. This time with a clockwise motion circle the working area until it becomes difficult to move the crystal or you feel that the area has had sufficient. As always, check your work by scanning or with your pendulum.

This method can be used for working on the person and their chakras but it is not necessary for sweeping the aura where one crystal is sufficient.

The end of the treatment

When you have completed the treatment, that is using either one or two crystals on a specific place and or a chakra balance and or an aura cleansing, you will need to end the treatment. The first part is to make sure your client is all right. First, run your hand down from head to toes asking for the chakras to be closed for going outside; this will ensure that the client is not open and vulnerable to outside influences. When they get up make sure they do it slowly and help them as necessary. Check that the client is in the here and now as described earlier by grounding them. Make sure they know that there may be changes to them, that memories from the past may come out or that they may feel different. Explain about the possibility of a healing crisis; reassure them that this is normal and safe. Also, tell them that they can contact you if they wish to say what has happened to them or to ask you questions. At this stage, much of this will not happen as you will only be working with friends and family, but it is still important to provide after-treatment support.

The final stage is for you. Ground yourself; shake your hands, touch them to the earth to remove any excess and unwanted energy. Thank your guides or energy sources for their help. Go and wash your hands in running water. And cleanse your crystals. Make sure you cleanse the working environment, too, by using smudge, candles or essential oils, and opening the window if possible.

EXERCISES

In a sense the whole of this unit is an exercise, so it will now be broken down into separate exercises. After completing exercises 1, 2 and 3 you should do one additional exercise and only one additional exercise on an individual person at any one time. Allow at least 24 hours between exercises on the same person. Try to repeat the exercises as many times as possible, on as many people as possible, all practice must be good. At the end of each session check the person you have been working on and go through your own finishing procedure as just described.

Exercise 1: Case history

Take a case history.

Exercise 2: Scanning

Go through your pre-treatment routine and then, using your hand(s), scan the individual and note down your findings.

Exercise 3: Pendulum

Use your pendulum to scan the body, again writing down your findings.

Exercise 4:

Only undertake this exercise if you find any areas that you feel require some work or if the client complains of a pain in a specific area. Use the instructions in this unit for using a single crystal and clear the area. Then replenish the energy using a single crystal.

Exercise 5: Chakra balance

Using one Clear Quartz crystal and the instructions given earlier undertake a chakra balance, remembering to close the chakras at the end by sweeping your hand from head to toe.

Exercise 6: Aura clearing

If you find a layer in the aura you feel requires clearing, use your single Clear Quartz point in sweeping movements as just described.

Exercise 7: Using two Clear Quartz points

Practice Exercises 4 and 5 using a pair of points.

UNIT 6 – CRYSTALS, CHAKRAS AND AURAS

This unit concentrates on working with the chakras. It will involve the use of different stones in different forms of layout. The first thing to do when beginning to use different crystals is make sure that you have an understanding of each type of crystal. If you have not already done so you will need to go through the exercises in Unit 3 to gain an inner understanding of Hematite, Carnelian, Citrine, Rose Quartz, Blue Lace Agate, Sodalite and Amethyst. To start with, tumbled stones are the best. They are easier both to obtain and identify. You will need one of each and they need to be about two to three centimetres in length and similar or smaller in width and about one to two centimetres in depth. Different crystals come in different ratios and availability. The Sodalite should be smaller as it will be placed on the forehead. We will be using some others but that should give you enough to get on with. Unfortunately, it is not possible to complete this work or this book in hours or days; it will take several months. However, the result is worth it; remember that in the UK a professional practitioner course takes a minimum of two years' part-time training.

Colours

In Unit 4, we looked at the seven major chakras, and each was given a colour. There is a certain amount of thought behind the colour and whether the given colours really relate to the chakra. In the west, the colours are somewhat arbitrary being taken from the rainbow spread. When we look at the properties of the chakras and of crystals that have the same colours, there is a reasonable correlation between them. That is not to say that every crystal of a given colour will be good for the chakra associated with that colour.

As we are learning, each particular type of crystal has certain properties. These can be applied to the chakras to help bring balance to the individual chakra and the whole system. If a particular chakra is already in balance the crystal will do no harm; if anything it may assist the other stones that are used in the balance layout. It is not necessary to use the complete set if you feel that certain chakras are all right. These two statements seem to contradict each other, but you will find that sometimes you will want to use the whole set, and sometimes just some of them; remember to trust your intuition.

Although the list given at the beginning of this unit is a chakra balance set, it is by no means the only set. Different people use different stones and some situations may indicate the use of one or more different stones as substitutes in the original set. The only rule is that you have studied the stone before using it on someone else.

Chakra balance: self-treatment

The basic chakra layout is normally a pleasant and beneficial experience for the client. A good idea is to try it on yourself first. Although laying the stones on can be a little awkward, it is worth persevering. So prepare your room and yourself. Make sure you have the crystals at hand. Lie down on your back, make sure you are comfortable and warm enough; your body temperature will change as you relax making you feel cold. Start with the Base Chakra: place the Hematite on the front of your body just above the genitals on the pubic bone. Next place the Carnelian on the Sacral Chakra. If you do not know exactly where your chakras are, return to Unit 5 and find them, for once you have identified them you will remember where they are.

After the Sacral, place the Citrine on the Solar Plexus Chakra, the Rose Quartz on the Heart Chakra and the Blue Lace Agate on the Throat Chakra. Next is the Sodalite on the Brow Chakra. Approach this one with care; it can be quite a shock to the system to suddenly have a crystal dropped on to it. Finally, place the Amethyst at the top of your head, probably on the cushion or pillow that your head is resting on. Place your arms by your sides and give yourself permission to relax and enjoy the treatment. At the same time allow yourself to monitor what is happening to you, try to remain as detached as possible. If any stones fall off, do not worry, let them be. Crystals will often know when they have completed their task and remove themselves from the area. After about 15 minutes, in your mind try to go to each chakra, starting at the Base Chakra and ask how it feels; would it like the crystal to remain for a little longer or would it like it removed. Often your whole system will be enjoying the sensation and will not want it to stop! The other possibility is that you may drift off to sleep. So, before you start, make sure you have enough time and set an alarm if you have later commitments.

If, after 20 minutes, you still do not want to remove them, make yourself the promise of repeating the exercise and take the crystals off, one at a time starting at the Crown Chakra and working down to the Base Chakra. Give yourself some time to come round, make sure you are grounded and, of course, cleanse your crystals. How do you feel? Write up your experiences in your journal and try the whole exercise again another day.

Chakra balance: other people

Working with other people is very similar to working on yourself except you are going to find out more about their chakras before you start using the crystals.

Starting procedure

Before you begin your start-up routine, prepare your client by briefly telling them what you are going to do. Have the client lie on their back and let them relax. Make sure they are comfortable and warm. Relax yourself and sit close to the client. The first action is just to look and observe the client. How are they lying? Does one area look different or stand out from the others? Do any parts look empty? Some of these questions may seem strange, but they will make sense as you get used to looking at the energy fields. Sometimes the differences are very small, so again, you must trust your intuition. If you do not think you are seeing anything, try looking slightly above or sideways, and not directly at the client.

The energy fields may appear in your peripheral vision. You can follow your thoughts with practical work including scanning and pendulum.

Scanning

Next is the scanning. Gently rub your hands together and slowly bring your scanning hand into the aura of the client until it is about six inches away from the body and above the Base Chakra. Start with the densest energy levels and work up to the highest. Slowly and gently move your hand around in the horizontal plain. Try moving your hand up and down; if you feel anything note how high you are above the body. What have you felt? If you do not feel anything, just relax and try again. There may be nothing to feel. Write down your finding. Later as you get used to working in this way you can remember all the results and then write them down.

Slowly move your hand up to the Sacral Chakra; again try circular movements and moving up and down. The reason for moving the hand is that it appears to be more sensitive when moved through the energy field, rather than just being static. Work up through the rest of the chakras, the Solar Plexus, Heart, Throat, Brow and Crown.

Having scanned all of the seven chakras, what are your findings, were there some that felt different to the others, what do you think this means? Were some at different heights? If so you need to find which layer of the aura; were all the feelings in the same layer or in different layers? From this information you can build up a picture of the individual, where they need extra help and where seems to be normal.

Pendulum scanning

The final diagnostic process is to use your pendulum and ask questions about each chakra and about what you have found so far. Remember that the questions need to have yes or no answers. Again, start at the Base Chakra and hold the pendulum two or three inches above the body. Give the pendulum time to function. Then try moving the pendulum closer to the body and then further away in stages. Write down your findings. Repeat this process over the other six chakras. There is a certain amount of information that you can get from the pendulum. You can ask it to show you the energy of the chakra, but as this is not a 'yes–no' question, so you will have to discover what the results mean.

One interpretation of the pendulum movements is if the chakra is functioning in a relatively normal way the pendulum will rotate, with a stronger rotation signifying a greater energy within the chakra and the related systems. The rotation can be in either direction. The rotation of chakras is sometimes supposed to relate to whether the individual is male or female and to alternate between chakras. You may find that it varies between individuals and within individuals and depends on their personal energy and physical cycles. If the pendulum swings across the body then it may be indicating that the chakra is not working properly and is blocking the energy flow through the body. A swing from head to toe may indicate that the chakra is neither accepting energy from the outside nor working properly but is not blocking the flow through the body. This shows one of the problems of working with the chakras, in that they have many functions and we are still in our infancy of discovering what they are and how they work. This will complete your search for information.

One way to utilise it is to draw a chart or a matrix. The chart can be a stick person with the chakras marked and your results written by the side. The matrix is a grid with the names of the chakras down the left hand side and columns and space for your results (see Figure 6.1).

Analysing the results

Look at your results; do all the methods used agree or are there differences, are all the differences related to an auric layer? What you are trying to do is build an energy picture of the person. Also, if they have mentioned any particular health problem, refer to what part of the body relates to which chakra; is that one of the chakras which has provided some form of reading? Try not to superimpose your intellectual thoughts onto the process, let your intuition or inner guide provide the relationships.

You now have lots of information, and in your first applications that may seem all you have got, lots of information. You still do not know how to apply it. As you undertake more treatments, you will

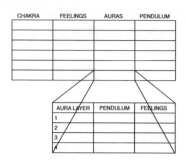

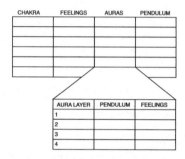

Figure 6.1   Chakras results matrix

begin to see and understand more. You will also become more sensitive; even if you think you are at the same level you will have moved on. For your first few treatments you will probably just place the stones, but as you become more experienced you will use more and more of the information you gain from the client.

Placing the crystals

Now to the application of the stones. Select your seven stones for the chakra balance. They are:

- Hematite for the Base Chakra
- Carnelian for the Sacral Chakra
- Citrine for the Solar Plexus Chakra
- Rose Quartz for the Heart Chakra
- Blue Lace Agate for the Throat Chakra

■ Sodalite for the Brow Chakra

■ Amethyst for the Crown Chakra.

If you have them and have worked with them, two Aventurine stones for the hands help with the overall balance and can feel soothing.

Starting at the Base Chakra place the Hematite on the pubic bone and the centre line of the body, next place the Carnelian on the Sacral Chakra, the Citrine on the Solar Plexus Chakra, the Rose Quartz on the Heart Chakra, the Blue Lace Agate on the Throat Chakra, the Sodalite on the Brow Chakra and the Amethyst behind the head. If you can, raise the Amethyst up on another cushion so that it is at about the same level as the Crown Chakra. It needs to be within two or three inches of the head.

Let the client be

Move away from the client, but be close enough so that you can observe their breathing and the chakras. Sometimes it is difficult to get the crystals to stay in place, particularly the Base and Heart Chakras, normally because of the shape of the body at these places. You may have to move clothing to form supports for the stones. Once you are satisfied they have a firm base but they fall off again let them be. The stones are better at knowing when their work is done than we are most of the time. Monitor your client: they may keep silent, or they may tell you what is happening in their body. If they feel strange, reassure them, if there is a marked reaction they may move and again if any stones fall off let them stay off. If the client starts to become emotional, you can hold their hand and reassure them and empathise with them, but keep it at that unless you are a trained counsellor.

Removing the crystals

After about 20 minutes scan over the crystals with your hand. How do the chakras feel? If you wish use your pendulum, ask whether it is a good time to remove each stone.

Depending on your results remove the stones from the Crown Chakra through to the Base. The Base Chakra or feet should always be the last stones removed as they help ground the individual.

Finally, if you have used them, remove the Aventurine from the hands. Let your client come round; they may have been asleep or in a near-sleep state. After a few minutes, say to them to come back to the room in their own time. Help them get up and sit them in a chair. Ask how they feel and try to obtain some feedback.

Make sure the person is grounded and safe to go out and that is the end of your session. Wash your hands and cleanse your room and crystals. Write up your notes.

Using Clear Quartz in the chakra balance

That was the standard chakra balance. It is possible to work in other ways with the chakras. The first takes the method just described and adds to it. This time instead of just sitting back, you will need your two Clear Quartz points. Get to the stage where you have just put your crystals on the chakras, and then work through the chakras in the following way: Starting at the Base Chakra, work over the Hematite stone and using your receiving hand with the crystal point facing towards your wrist work in an anti-clockwise manner pulling out any negative energy. Your sending hand should be away from the body pointing down towards the earth. Ask that any negative energy be transmuted into positive energy for the good of all. Keep rotating until you feel as if the negative energy has been cleared. Reverse the process and apply positive energy by placing your sending hand with the crystal pointing towards the fingers over the chakra and rotating in a clockwise direction. Your receiving hand should be palm up with the crystal pointing towards the wrist. Allow the positive energy to flow for as long as necessary. When you have finished each chakra scan or use your pendulum to check the state of the chakra after working on it. Write down your findings. Move on to the Sacral Chakra, repeating the process as necessary. Compare the amount of removal and replacement you need to do with your findings from the scanning and pendulum. Work up through the rest of the chakras finishing with the Crown Chakra.

After working on all the chakras check through them and if there are still any that do not feel quite right repeat the work on those. When you are satisfied, remove the gemstones, starting at the

Crown Chakra and work down to the Base Chakra. Give the client time to recover and if possible gain feedback from them. Make sure they are well grounded and feel fine. Ground yourself as necessary, cleanse your crystals, room, and yourself, and finally write up your notes.

A modified Clear Quartz addition

A slightly faster version of this work, and one to try as you become more experienced is to refer back to your findings about the energy of the chakras and only work on those that indicated that something was abnormal. Still place a relevant stone on every chakra, but only work with the Clear Quartz points on those chakras that you found to be out of balance in some way. When working like this it is very important to scan over all the chakras afterwards because your work on one chakra may cause changes in the others, in particular those either side of it and the related chakra. The related chakras are as follows: Base–Crown; Sacral–Brow; Solar Plexus–Throat.

Different layouts

There are, of course, many ways of working with the chakras. Two that can be very useful are a calming layout and an energising layout. Before applying either of these, check the chakras for being out of balance, if there is nothing seriously wrong then proceed. If the chakras appear way out of balance, consider using Clear Quartz to bring them towards balance before moving on to the next stage. When you feel that the chakras are ready, apply one of the following layouts. The first is the calming, loving layout. It requires at least seven Rose Quartz stones, preferably ten. However, it is possible to undertake this layout with only one Rose Quartz.

Rose Quartz layout

The client should already be lying down on their back and you have already checked the chakras. Place a Rose Quartz on the Heart Chakra and, if you only have one Rose Quartz, this is your layout!

Next, place a Rose Quartz at the Base Chakra and also at the Crown Chakra. Follow this with Rose Quartz at the Sacral and Brow Chakras. Try to use a small crystal on the Brow Chakra, as it can be extremely sensitive. Now place Rose Quartz on the Solar Plexus and Throat Chakras. If you have sufficient stones place a Rose Quartz below the feet and one in each hand. Let the person lie there for about 20 minutes. Keep the room warm as they may go into a deeply relaxed state. Scan over the client to make sure everything is all right and remove the Rose Quartz from the Crown to the Throat, the Solar Plexus, Sacral, and Base Chakras, from below the feet and the hands and finally from the Heart Chakra.

Check with the client and really make sure that they are grounded. This sort of treatment can be very calming and relaxing.

Enlivening layout

The opposite form of treatment is the enlivening layout. The idea of this is to allow the individual to approach life calmly but with enthusiasm. One crystal that is known for its vitality is Citrine, but a Citrine layout is likely to be too much for most people. Instead, there will only be five or seven crystals used, Citrine, Hematite, two Clear Quartz points and three Rose Quartz stones. As always, check that the chakras are in reasonable order then apply the crystals to the chakras. Start at the Base Chakra with the Hematite, then one Clear Quartz point at the Crown Chakra with the point towards the head, place the Citrine on the Solar Plexus Chakra and the Rose Quartz on the Heart Chakra. The other two Rose Quartz crystals are placed in the hands. To increase the energy of the Citrine use the other Clear Quartz. Hold it above the Citrine with the point downwards. Check that there is no negative energy to remove by rotating in an anti-clockwise manner and then rotate clockwise for about a minute, then stop but keep the crystal pointing at the Citrine. Repeat the rotation twice more then check the chakra.

After 20 minutes check all of the chakras and if you feel they have had enough, remove the crystals from the Crown Chakra down. Give the client time to recover and ask for feedback.

Other layouts

There are other ways of using crystals with chakras. It is possible to use seven stones of the same type. When doing this you are applying the essence of one particular chakra to all the other chakras, which, of course, have parts of that chakra within them. If this is done with a series of different stones over time, it can assist in bringing the person into balance and for them to access parts of themselves that may have been locked away for years. The choice of the type of crystal is dependent on why the treatment is needed. In general, if there is one chakra that is out of balance to the others then choose a crystal that relates to that chakra. Further layouts are discussed later. As always, try these layouts on yourself first so that you can assess whether they are what is required.

EXERCISES

This unit is an exercise in itself so work through the following methods of working with the chakras.

1 Sit with each of the following crystals; if possible spend longer with them. Hematite, Carnelian, Citrine, Rose Quartz, Blue Lace Agate, Sodalite and Amethyst. If you intend to use any of the other stones mentioned elsewhere such as Garnet, Smoky Quartz or Tourmalated Quartz meditate with these as well.

2 Practise the basic chakra layout on yourself.

3 Practise the various ways of feeling energy around the chakras on as many people as possible.

4 Try the chakra balance layout on other people.

5 Try the chakra balance with the additional use of Clear Quartz points.

6 Try the calming chakra work.

7 Try the invigorating chakra exercise.

UNIT 7 – ADVANCED LAYOUTS

This unit deals with further layouts on the client and Unit 8 looks at the use of crystals around the person. There is, of course, considerable overlap between the two units, but work through each one separately before bringing them together. In many ways, this unit builds upon the work carried out in the preceding units. Anything that is repeated is to assist in making the unit complete and it also acts as revision.

What is a layout?

The first question to address is what a layout is. The simple answer is any crystals placed on or around the individual being worked upon. We have already tried several specific crystal layouts on the chakras. The earlier exercises started with one or two clear points of the body, then basic balancing layouts, calming and energising, which were then enhanced with Clear Quartz; scanning and pendulum analysis was also undertaken. Next these ideas are going to be combined so that you can produce layouts for each individual, not from a set pattern but what is actually required. You will need additional crystals but do not rush out and buy them yet. Read through the unit and see what you really need.

The person you are working with determines the layouts you are going to use. If they are basically fit and well, but overstretched you may feel that they need a simple grounding and relaxing treatment. A part of any treatment must be the time the person has lying down, not able to go anywhere, no phone to answer, no computer to use, nothing to do but just lie there. They cannot move very far, they can still think but the ambiance of the room tends to enable them just to be in the now.

Additional crystal places

There are many ways that you can place patterns of crystals on the body. The decisions that have to be made are what crystals should be used and where should they be placed. We have looked at the chakras and seen that each chakra is linked to physical, mental and spiritual parts of the body. We can utilise this in producing a layout by taking the chakras as the starting point. You will know what condition they are in having scanned them or used your pendulum. There are a lot of other places that can also be used to place crystals. Although we will deal with crystals off the body in the next unit, the first new position is below the feet. The only other way of working in this area would be to tape them to the soles of the feet. The stone is placed at the bottom of each foot or between the feet. This is an excellent site for grounding and for encouraging the flow of energy through the body. In general, the heavier stones are placed here, but of course, there are exceptions.

Working up the body the next new place is at the knees. This is like a halfway point between the Base Chakra and the feet. When grounding energy is low or missing, this place may be blocked or in need of some assistance. The type of stone that can be placed here is one that encourages the flow of energy, such as a small Clear Quartz point or, as mentioned later, Smoky Quartz.

The next positions are the two groin points. These can be used in addition to, or instead of the Base Chakra. It can be difficult to place crystals on the pubic bone for the Base Chakra, and if crystals will not stay there, the groin points are easier to use. These points are where the top of the thigh meets the pubic bone. There may be a small hollow. They also have their own role to play. The final new points are at the shoulders, about two to three inches down from the top. This is a good place to provide support. All of these additional points are shown in Figure 7.1.

This now gives a reasonable coverage of the body with known places, and with a given set of stones, you can develop a different layout for each person you work with, if it is needed. Although the places to put the stones are given and the type of crystals you have are limited in number the possible combination is enormous.

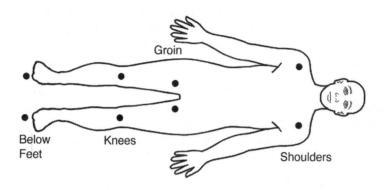

Figure 7.1   Additional points

Where to place the crystals

As always, before starting work go back to the beginning and after preparing yourself, taking a case history, scanning and/or using your pendulum which gives you the areas that need working upon you have to decide what crystals to use and where to put them. This is best approached through a process of elimination. The first place to start is by asking why this person wants a treatment. In the first cases you work on, the answer may be because you asked them if you could practise on them. However, if there is a reason then you will need to consider the type of crystals that will assist with that situation and how this fits in with the scan you have carried out.

A general way of assisting physical problems is to place a ring of crystals around the area to help remove negative energy and then replace these after a while with a ring of beneficial crystals. A ring could be as small as two stones although four would be more effective. The type of stones to use really does depend on what you are trying to do. It is important to think about what is happening to the person and understand what any particular crystal does.

Using colour

Sometimes a simple guide can help you make the first few decisions before your intuition takes over. One guide is colour. By looking at what the person needs and using colour as the first thought, whether they need hot or cold, energy or calm, can start to provide a clue as to which crystals to use. In this unit, we will use those crystals involved in the basic chakra balance. Other stones will be considered later in the book. Many crystal books associate certain stones with specific illnesses and body parts. Here the intention is to try to apply the energy of the stone that best suits the loss or damage to the energy source of the person under consideration.

As a starting point, we will take a simple example, after that the stones in the chakra set will be discussed. Then, you will need to make the decision as to what stone to place where. As you become more proficient, you will also start placing stones elsewhere on the body. The first example and colour use starts with a physical problem of swelling and redness. The normal idea is to try to reduce the inflammation. To reduce the redness should you add more of the same colour, a red crystal, or use a cooling colour such as blue and an appropriate blue crystal. Most forms of using colour apply the opposite colour; it is like applying something cold to an injury caused by heat, cold water to a burn, or in the opposite case gentle heat to a cold extremity. In addition, certain colours are known for their energetic properties without having to consider opposites.

Do all blue stones work in the same way? If they did then there would not need to have a wide collection of different crystals. You would be able to work with as few as six different crystals. Therefore, to diffuse redness and swelling consider a blue crystal. At the moment your light blue crystal is Blue Lace Agate, and this is a very good cooling stone. The other blue crystal is Sodalite, and although this would work it has a darker energy that is not as effective at cooling.

Physical or emotional

The next question to consider is what is causing the hot area. Is it purely physical, in which case the application of the blue crystal to the red area would seem appropriate, or is there an emotional aspect involved? If there is an emotional aspect, from where within the chakra system is it manifesting? This may have been identified in your scanning and then a stone that may deal with such issues should be placed at the identified chakra. Cool the hot area, but apply a crystal that relates to the emotional aspects to the chakra, a Rose Quartz or Aventurine may be appropriate.

Where there may be more than one influence, consider a mixture of two or three stones within the same spectrum. These stones will be placed around the appropriate chakra. Having applied your knowledge of crystals to the symptom and possibly to at least part of the cause there is the rest of the person to consider in this layout as well. During your initial analysis you may have discovered imbalance in other areas that are either part of other issues or a compensation for the prime problem. If so, you will need to place crystals around or over these. The same applies to the chakras; any that were blocked or low in energy need appropriate action, so that they too can be started on their path to balance.

The colours and the crystals

Other situations will call for different colours; two that are often needed are yellow and orange. These vibrant colours can be used to promote energy and enthusiasm, just consider what happens to people's emotions on a bright summer's day. They can be used to combat both physical and mental areas that are sluggish or slow. Carnelian is our basic orange stone; this stone has a strong energy that can be applied to assist in generating movement. If someone is having difficulty with the basic creativity and energy of life then try using Carnelian. It is normally associated with the Sacral Chakra but can be used at the throat to assist with expression. It could be placed over parts of the digestive system if it is not as effective as it should be. In all cases, it is important to try to find the root cause as well as treating the symptom. Be cautious of using Carnelian where there is a history of high blood pressure.

The yellow stone in our basic set is Citrine; this is also energetic but at a higher level. If someone is suffering from a sluggish mind then try a small Citrine on the Brow or Crown Chakra. The energy from Citrine can be very clear and concise. There are many colours of both these stones, in particular Citrine which may be natural or created by heating Amethyst. The natural Citrine tends to be lighter with a brighter energy, whereas the created Citrine is darker with a more intense, lower level energy. Citrine can also be used to assist people to move on, to get out of the rut that they find themselves in. When used at the Solar Plexus Chakra it can assist the individual to take up their own innate power and will.

The pink of Rose Quartz can be applied to all parts of the body where a gentle but powerful caring energy is needed. This energy is of Universal Love, but sometimes it may produce extreme results where the loss of love within the individual is great. The inflow from the crystal can help bring out the pain and hurt from the past in both this life and others. This sort of reaction is rare and is normally brought about by crystals that open the pathway, not by applying Universal Love. A complete basic layout on the chakras, shoulders, hands, groin, and feet can be accomplished using Rose Quartz as discussed earlier. This can be a very rewarding and beautiful treatment. Areas of the body that have been, and still are, suffering from a chronic condition may benefit from a ring of Rose Quartz, particularly where you suspect that the cause of the condition is not entirely physical. It can be used after surgery, and although pink, it should not add to the redness, as the love quality is very strong.

The green of Aventurine is a general healing colour. Aventurine often has sparks of light within it, which assist the stone in bringing about a general balance as well as a very positive forward-looking energy. It is a gentle general stone. Beware of some other green stones, as they can be very powerful, and very good at opening the energy channels related to emotions. Malachite can draw out deep emotions and should always be used with a crystal that can support the client when this happens.

The light blue stone in our chakra set is Blue Lace Agate. This is usually a very pale blue with bands of white or very pale grey. The energy from this stone can work very well with problems that produce symptoms involving red swelling, particularly where there are mucous membranes or dampness, for instance, in the throat. It can be applied anywhere on the body to help alleviate red swelling. Remember that not all swelling is hot and red and placing a Blue Lace Agate on a swelling that is cold, white and hard may be counter productive.

The second blue stone in the set is the dark blue Sodalite; this can have white streaks in it, which provide lightness to the dark. This stone is noted for its calming effect, particularly on the mind. It acts with a stillness that is useful in meditation and in treatments. It produces this stillness without slowing down the ability to think. Because it seems to reduce the extraneous thoughts, it may even improve the ability to think clearly. The energy seems to be deeper than required to counter the effects brought about by redness. However, because of the calming effect it may be useful with high blood pressure.

The Crown Chakra stone is the Amethyst, and it is a beautiful colour in all its manifestations. Amethyst, as you have probably discovered, comes in a whole spectrum of purples from very pale lavender through to the darkest purple. In all of its colours, it provides a subtle energy, a spark of life. The purple colours are very much a connection to the spiritual part of people and it is normally associated with this area. It can be held in the hands or placed near the Heart Chakra to bring spiritual love to the heart. It also provides us with inner strength to deal with all of life's situations by connecting us to our spiritual source. Purple is also used for protection, possibly because of the link to the spiritual as we often call upon our god, goddess, or spiritual being for assistance in moments of crisis. Amethyst can be very useful when dealing with all sorts of loss, from death to separation.

The final stone in our set is the Hematite. A stone of great weight and used for grounding; silver in colour it can be used to combat trauma. This is because of its grounding properties and as has been said grounding is very important in the relief of panic. It is also associated with the blood system of the body, from whence it derives its name. The grounding colour is often taken as black. Some grounding stones are black. Black can also be very protective as this colour tends to absorb energy. Consider how black absorbs the sun's energy, keeping it for itself and, in a sense, protecting anything beyond it. Other grounding stones are red or green. It depends on what the requirement is.

The links between the colours and the crystals should help in making the decision about which crystals to place where. If you are not sure you can ask the crystal that you feel should be used or use your pendulum to make the choice between two stones.

The holistic approach

The important aspect to consider all of the time is that the treatment should be holistic. It is important to take into account the whole person each time you apply a crystal. The best way to work is to consider the whole treatment, the whole layout before applying a single stone. Collect all the stones that you want to use as you look at each aspect that has been drawn to your attention, and when you have built up the layout in your mind, and it feels balanced, apply them. The order of application should be to the feet first, then any crystals that you are going to use on the head, then along the chakras starting at the Base Chakra and working up, and finally any other places you need to work on. This gives the energy system a chance to flow before addressing specific problems. The time is only seconds but when looked at from a holistic idealism the treatment starts by addressing the cause before the symptom.

If ever there is a doubt about whether to use a stone or not, the best thing is not to use it. The idea of covering someone with lots of crystals also seems strange. Remember that this work is with very subtle energies. To apply too many crystals is like having your own power station for each appliance in the house: it would overload the network. Keep the layouts as simple as possible. Not every chakra always needs a crystal. The chakra balance layout is very specific but can be altered as necessary. Try to keep an open mind about which crystals to use where. The basic set of chakra crystals can be applied in many different ways to produce many different layouts. All of these can be kept simple.

Because you are making the decision of which crystal to place where, it is important that you ask the client for feedback. Give them permission at the beginning of the session to let you know if they feel strange or if they feel changes within themselves. If they do you will have to decide whether to keep the same layout or whether to change one or more crystals. Try to let the crystals complete their work. Often strange feelings are caused by shifts in the energy fields. Occasionally strange feelings are caused by the crystal beginning its work, or because of the interaction of several crystals when the person is not in balance. It may seem strange to give the person permission, but often the client does not know what is expected of them. It also helps to relax them as, in a sense, they feel that they are in control and can say if they do not like what is happening.

Additional Clear Quartz points

Basic crystal layouts can be augmented by the use of other crystals between the major stones. The most common practise is the use of Clear Quartz points. Their function is many from providing a source of energy to acting as a channel for other forms of energy to flow along. On any layout, a Clear Quartz point can be held above one or more of the other crystals to increase its effectiveness. Using a single Clear Quartz crystal with the point aimed at the crystal on the body, rotate it in an anti-clockwise direction to remove negative energy. To increase the effect of the crystal on the body point the crystal towards the stone and rotate in a clockwise direction. While doing either of these visualise the flow of energy out of or into the crystal. As always, let your intuition tell you when to stop. Another way of removing negative energy is to use the quartz crystal like a hook or a needle to get underneath the negative energy and pull it out. Although this is not a layout, it can form an important part of a treatment.

Removing negative energy with Clear Quartz

This can be done in two ways. The first is to use the Clear Quartz crystal like a small knife cutting out a bad spot from a vegetable. Working above the body use the crystal to cut around the area you wish to remove. If necessary visualise the energy coming out of the point like a fine beam of light that can cut through the energy layer several inches below it. Work in an anti-clockwise manner going around the area several times and lift out the energy and immediately send it to the earth to be neutralised. An important consideration when removing energy like this is you. Make sure you have placed a protective cocoon around you before starting this work, otherwise, the negative energy could take up residence in your own energy fields.

The second way is to scoop the negative energy out with the point of the Clear Quartz. This is similar to trying to spoon runny honey out of a jar; the crystal has to be twisted round with the wrist and the energy hooked onto the crystal and pulled out. Again, ensure that the energy is sent quickly to the earth for neutralisation. Which method you use depends what the energy feels like. If, when you were scanning the person, you could feel a thick mass above the body, the second may be very effective. If you could feel a very specific negative area in the body then the first method may be better. If you do not know which to use, you could always try both and see which one is more effective.

Clear Quartz in the layout

The third way to use Clear Quartz crystals is to place them between other crystals in a layout. They help encourage the natural energy of the person to travel and assist the energy of the other crystals in the layout flow up and down the body. The point of the crystal is placed in the direction in which you want the energy to flow. If you feel that an individual has too much head energy and is not grounded, you can apply a layout that assists in the grounding process. At the very basic level this consists of a Hematite at the Base Chakra and at the feet and a Rose Quartz at the Heart Chakra for support. You could also add a Citrine or Amethyst pointing towards the feet at the Crown Chakra to provide an additional source of energy to move down the body. Then, place one or more Clear Quartz points with the points aimed towards the feet on the centre line of the body between the Throat and Heart Chakras, and between the Heart and Base Chakras. Additional Clear Quartz can be placed just above each knee with the termination towards the feet.

Monitor the flow of energy with your hand or pendulum. When you feel that any blockages have been cleared and that there is a better connection between the top of the body and the bottom remove the Clear Quartz and then the other crystals starting at the top and working down. Afterwards check them again and if possible gain feedback.

Another crystal to use to assist in bringing people out of their heads and into their body is Smoky Quartz. This can be used at the bottom of the feet pointing away from the body, at the knees pointing towards the feet and at the groin areas pointing down towards the legs. As well as helping to move the energy, Smoky Quartz also helps change the pattern that is causing the imbalance, thus supporting the individual with their change (see Figure 7.2).

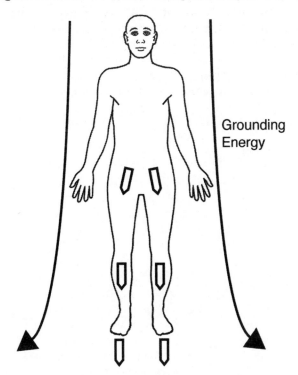

Grounding Energy

Figure 7.2   Grounding energy

Using double-terminated crystals

Sometimes the energy flow between the chakras is dormant when it should be a two way process. Although each chakra is independent, they are also interconnected and do not function in an effective way unless they have energy flowing from the chakras that surround them. If this is the case, try using a double-terminated Clear Quartz crystal. These have points on both ends, which helps the energy flow in two directions. The terminations are not always perfect or symmetrical which in some ways adds to their charm. If you consider the links between the Throat and the Heart Chakras are weak, place a double-terminated Clear Quartz between the Blue Lace Agate at the throat and the Rose Quartz at the heart. As always, monitor the reaction. Double-terminated Clear Quartz crystals also work well at the groin and between the groin, knees and feet. They are also effective between the lower five chakras (see Figure 7.3). It is not easy to apply additional crystals above the Throat Chakra. The energy levels are very high in the area of the head and the Brow Chakra and the Crown Chakra are normally well connected, and there are not many flat places for the crystals.

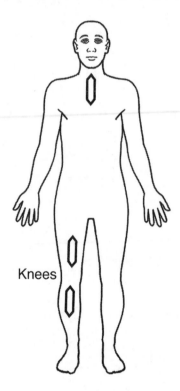

Knees

Figure 7.3   Double-terminated points

The flow of energy in the body is an ever-moving pattern. In addition, it is not always easy to decide in which direction it should be going. In the last case we saw just now where you feel that an individual is not grounded and they are spending too much time in their head, the suggestion was to use a layout that brought some of the possible excess energy down from the head to the lower part of the body, where the energy is depleted or sluggish. It is just as possible that there could be a blockage that is stopping the base energy from rising, in which case the lower areas would be filled with energy and the top ones depleted of earth energy. Here the Clear Quartz would be used with the points towards the head. A third case would be where the person had energy in both the top and bottom of their body but it was not flowing. This is the time for double-terminated Clear Quartz as it aids the flow in both directions.

If you do not have any double-terminated crystals, you can use two ordinary Clear Quartz points of similar size, and place them long side by long side with points at opposite ends, or with their blunt ends facing each other.

The meridian system

One of the ways in which energy is carried around the body is by the meridian system. This consists of a series of very fine channels that are all interconnected to form a single loop. It travels up and down the body, head, arms and legs several times with each length representing the energy of different parts of the body. This pattern can be very useful in developing layouts for individuals. Meridians and their properties were identified by the Chinese and possibly the Indians or Tibetans before that. We already have a little knowledge of the system, as the chakras are part of it. Each meridian has a series of points that are charted; each of these relates to a part of the body and can affect the function of that part of the body. Practitioners of acupuncture, acupressure and shiatsu use this process; they use needles or pressure on selected points identified by their diagnosis to assist the flow of energy around the body and the removal of disease caused by under- or over-activity.

Knowledge of the meridians can be used with crystals to help change the energy flow within the body. It must be stated that knowledge of the meridians and Chinese medicine take years to learn and understand. At this stage, they can be talked about and one or two points may be used but to make the most of their actions a full study should be undertaken. If, after study, you find a blockage occurring along a meridian or at a particular point, small Clear Quartz crystals and other crystals can be placed along the meridian to encourage the flow of energy. The second method uses a single Clear Quartz point in a similar way to the work on the chakras. The Clear Quartz point is used to discharge and recharge the meridians and certain points along them. The quartz crystal can also be used to trace the meridian. A pendulum can be used to find out the path of the meridian and the place of the blockage when necessary.

The conclusion of this unit has to be that although it would be possible to provide sets of crystal layouts, these would not necessarily be what is needed. The idea of the unit is to encourage you to discover more about your client and more about your crystals; then to try to bring the two together.

EXERCISES

The exercises for this unit are to go through the different methods described and to try as many as possible on yourself to understand how they feel. Go through the unit and try placing appropriate crystals on points that you have not used before. These include below the feet, the knees, shoulders and the groin areas.

When you obtain a double-terminated crystal find out about it by meditating with it, then try placing it on yourself in various places to obtain an idea of how it moves energy.

If you have a physical problem, try devising a layout to assist.

Try these on people who do not mind being experimented on. Make sure you tell them that this is practice and obtain as much feedback as possible.

UNIT 8 – USING CRYSTALS IN OTHER WAYS

The last unit looked at how to develop crystal layouts on the person; this unit goes beyond that, to examine the process of putting crystals around the person. There are four major categories in this unit: the first deals with patterns and grids around the individual and is probably the most important. We then look at the use of crystals in the healing room including under the healing couch; how to use crystal wands in the aura and with layouts; and finally at the use of crystals in jewellery.

The crystal grid

A simple way to use crystals off the body during a treatment is to place a certain number in a specific pattern around the person. They are then bathed in the energy of those crystals. This is normally achieved using a set of four, six, eight or more stones. There are those practitioners who use a large number of stones in complex patterns, some of which can have hundreds of crystals in them. We will use a small number in a few basic patterns. The effect is greatest if the pattern is of a particular shape. The shape is based on Sacred Geometry. Sacred Geometry is the study of shapes that increase or enhance the way in which energy moves. Certain buildings have shapes that enhance their energy flows. Certain symbols have shapes that enhance the energy flows. If this is applied to crystals then the energy flow of the crystals is enhanced and the benefit to the client can be increased.

There are certain shapes that have been used through the ages. The first is the simple equal-armed cross. This has been in use as a sacred symbol for many thousands of years by many different cultures. The Christianised version has the longer lower limb.

Where I live, in the southwest of England, there are stone crosses at the sides of roads and many of these are of the old equal form often with a circle around them. To use this shape in crystal healing place the four crystals in a cross pattern around the client. This can be one at the head, one at the feet and one on each side. Try to make sure that the crystals are equidistant from a central point. That is the first pattern and the next question is what stones to use here. In these layouts, the crystals are all the same type and if at all possible of similar size. The type of stone depends what the intention of the healing session is. If it is to provide comfort in time of emotional upset then either Rose Quartz or Amethyst may produce a good effect. In fact, you could combine the two and make two four-pointed crosses. First, place the four Rose Quartz crystals as just described; then place the four Amethysts in a cross in the spaces left by the Rose Quartz, so that the eight stones form a circle around the client. This form of combination and shape will give a greater amount of healing than the separate stones.

You can use the stones that you feel are needed. Just remember that the effect can be very powerful, far greater than the use of the separate crystals. This form of layout can be used either as a separate self-contained treatment or as part of a treatment with stones on the body and other activities. One of the benefits of these grids is that they are easy to test on yourself. You will need to work on the floor so that you can have the crystals at the same height as you are. Place the crystals in the required shape, lie down in the middle of them and enjoy the experience.

One of the other main shapes that can be used is the six-pointed star. Often associated with the Star of David this is also an ancient symbol used by a large variety of people. It is also making a comeback in the many logos used by all sorts of New Age and complementary health organisations. It is important to get the stones placed as accurately as possible so that they are equally spaced around a circle with one stone at the feet and one at the head, leaving two on each side. With this shape, another option is to use terminated crystals; these can be of a variety of types and can be used with the point towards the person or the point away from the person. This shape is made of two triangles, one bringing in the spiritual energy and the other the grounding energy.

When the crystals are placed with points out, they will help remove negative energy from the person and their aura. For this you can use Clear Quartz points or Smoky Quartz points. Smoky Quartz has two major properties and is a potent healer: it is a good grounding stone, although not as pulling as Hematite, and it has a lighter feel about it partly as it is a quartz stone and also, unless it has been treated, it has a light colour. Some Smoky Quartz is irradiated Amethyst and this can be very dark indeed. Smoky Quartz is good for helping remove negative energies at the physical, emotional and mental levels. The nice thing about it is that it does not leave a hole because it replaces the removed negative energy with an optimistic positive energy. Having been used for removing the negative side, it can be quickly cleansed to remove any remaining negative energy and turned so that the points now face in towards the client providing a gentle replacement of energy.

If you use Clear Quartz points the energy will be sharper and the extraction not so gentle or so much on the emotional level. Clear Quartz is a very powerful healer and when formed into a sacred shape its power is intensified. It is known to transform and amplify energy at a wide range of frequencies, which makes a good general purpose stone to use for removing negative energy; after which it may prove more beneficial to combine the Clear Quartz with another stone to induce the required positive energy. By using the six points you could have three Clear Quartz points and three Rose Quartz lumps, as there are very few terminated Rose Quartz stones available, alternating around the circle. This will give a strong, but loving energy that should bring vitality and peace to the client. Another option would be a combination of Amethyst points and Clear Quartz or Citrine points. All of these examples would be used after clearing with clear points and they would have their terminations towards the client.

Many combinations and patterns can be used. Try as many as you can on yourself and notice the difference they can make and the difference between the different crystals and combination of crystals. A useful aid is a template. On a white or pale colour sheet draw a large circle with a makeshift pair of compasses, a skewer, a piece of string and an indelible pen. Then mark the points for the four, six and eight points around the circle. If you are able, you can decorate these in a suitable manner. This can then be used as a template to position the crystals in the right place. This is very useful when trying the layouts on yourself. It can also be rather special for other people. Beware of using strong colours as the energy of the colour may interfere with the crystals and the receiver.

Layouts are not always possible for a variety of reasons. Another way to use crystals away from the body and to enhance a treatment is to position them strategically in the workroom. When you use this method, it is important to remember to cleanse them regularly as they can pick up all sorts of psychic debris. One simple way is to place a single Clear Quartz crystal in each corner of the room with the point towards the working area. If the room and the furniture permit it is also possible to set up a permanent grid of Clear Quartz points. If you work on a couch that is off the floor then this method can be very useful if the grid is on a similar level to the couch. Other crystals can also be placed around the room. Several pieces of Rose Quartz helps the room feel relaxed and caring and Aventurine can assist in keeping the integrity of the room as it is a gentle but effective healer working on energies to assist in creating a positive balance (see Figure 8.1).

Figure 8.1   Crystals in a room

Three-dimensional grids

Two adventurous ways of placing crystals in your workroom are by creating a three-dimensional matrix and, along similar ideas, creating a crystal pyramid. The three-dimensional matrix is a sacred geometric figure which instead of being in just the horizontal plane is also in two or more vertical planes. The simplest one to make is to use four points in a cross shape in the horizontal plane and add one crystal above the centre point at the same distance from the centre, and one crystal below at the same distance from the centre. You should then lie in this sphere of crystals with your head and feet near crystals. This is the simplest design. If you can try it then do so.

The next simplest shape is the six-pointed star. This requires a few more crystals, about 30 crystals depending on how it is built, and some way of holding them all together. The answer seems to remain with the cross shape as these can be balanced on furniture and the top crystal hung from the ceiling. The more complex shapes can be constructed using copper wire and garden canes, but it is not the easiest of tasks. The use of metals with crystals brings in a different aspect that cannot be covered here, because metals are conductors they change the energy flow of the crystals.

Crystal pyramids

The other idea is the crystal pyramid. This has two versions depending on the resources available. The first requires 12 Clear Quartz points and the second requires 16 Clear Quartz points. Copper wire also comes in handy; it needs to be thick enough to stay as shaped but thin enough to be easily bent. The nice thing about the pyramid is that it can be positioned anywhere and moved again. It is extremely portable.

The first version does not have a top, just four corners. The top is imagined and is where the energy of the four upward-pointing crystals meets. Each corner is made from three Clear Quartz crystals. One crystal represents the bottom edge of the pyramid, the second represents the second bottom edge and is at right angles to the first, and the third represents the corner edge of the pyramid and is at approximately 60° from the floor and bisects the other two crystals. All the points are away from the corner and towards the middle. These are constructed by wrapping one piece of copper wire around all three crystals. This is repeated so that there are four of these sets of crystals. These are then placed on the floor at the corners of a square, the corners of the room or other places where they will be safe. They are rather hard if you stand on them! Try to make sure that the top of the pyramid is still within your room. Also consider what is above you as the energy from the pyramid and the upward-pointing crystals can be very powerful.

The other version of the pyramid consists of the same sets of crystals for the base plus four crystals wired together with points outwards and all the bases together for the peak of the pyramid. This is suspended so that the crystals line up with those upward-pointing ones on the floor. In case you are wondering whether it is correct, each crystal point does have a point aiming towards it. These pyramids are wonderful places for meditating and for working in.

Other ways of placing crystals in rooms

If you use a therapist's couch or worktable you can also keep crystals under the couch on the floor or on a table or even taped to the underside of your worktable. Clusters of crystals can be very effective under the worktable, either Clear Quartz or Amethyst. A lump of Rose Quartz at the corners can also be of great assistance. If your worktable is of a permanent nature and not folded away each day you can have additional platforms or pockets attached to take crystals. These can be useful to put client-specific crystals into. If you feel that someone needs protection and grounding, a piece of Black Tourmaline in each corner may be of excellent value. Alternatively, Smoky Quartz crystals pointing towards the floor may help. By having these facilities you add another dimension to your work.

Crystal wands

All of these suggestions have been about using the crystals in a static manner, so now we will look at using crystals off the client in a more active way. The use of Clear Quartz points has been discussed; this next part adds a new dimension to that work. Although you can use any crystal around the client, one of the best resources is the wand. The crystal wand is not a naturally formed crystal. It has been cut and polished so that it has six sides, a domed or flat base and a pointed top. It is a very neat looking crystal. The main advantage is that it can be made from crystal types that do not have naturally occurring large terminated crystals, as well as those that do. This means that you can have a Rose Quartz wand, a Fluorite wand, plus smooth-sided crystals of those that do produce naturally terminated crystals including Clear Quartz and Amethyst.

Take time to choose your crystal wands, they can be of great value and because they have polished surfaces they are lovely to hold and meditate with. When you first get your wand, pay particular attention to cleansing it as it has been through a considerable amount of trauma. They are cut from large pieces of stone and then polished with various grades of abrasive material to produce a beautiful object. So, caring, cleansing and charging are very important to help produce a very useful tool. Also, be careful of the points as they are easily chipped.

These wands can be used in several ways. The most important are for removing unwanted energy, activating other crystals and for the auric massage.

Removing negative energy with a wand

There are two main methods of using a wand for removing unwanted junk, both of which we have talked about before. As a revision, those ideas will now be repeated. The first idea is to use the wand like a knife and cut out the unwanted energy, a form of psychic surgery. Hold the wand with the point towards the body and a few inches away from the body and use an anti-clockwise rotation to cut away the unwanted energy. When you have circled around several times lift that energy out and send it to the earth for transformation. It is important that you protect yourself during these types of manoeuvres as the negative energy may be looking for another host. The second method is to use the point like a hook and do just that: hook the negative energy out and away, again sending it to earth for transformation. In general, a Clear Quartz wand is the most effective at removing unwanted energy. If you have a Smoky Quartz wand, that can be very helpful as well. The Smoky Quartz tends not to be as sharp and hard as the Clear Quartz. The benefit of using a wand for this work is that, depending on size, it fits very comfortably into the hand and is unlikely to cut your fingers.

Adding positive energy with a wand

When it comes to replacing removed or lost energy the different wands are wonderful. The benefit is that you can direct the flow of crystal energy much more accurately with the wand than with a polished stone. It can be either held over the place under consideration or slowly circled in a clockwise direction, spiralling it in towards the body as it is circled. The rounded end of the wand can be used to seal the place that has been worked upon. This can be very helpful where you have had to remove a lot of negative or unwanted energy, like bringing the edges of a wound together and helping them to form a new skin. Gently circle the wand with the round end towards the body in clockwise direction until you feel that it is sealed.

Clearing the aura and auric massage

The next way of using a wand is as a massage tool. This helps place the energy of the crystal into the auric layers and it can also be used to remove unwanted energy sludge from the auric layer. The wand is now held so that one of the long sides is parallel to the body. How you hold it depends on the size of the wand and the size of your hands. There are two choices: the first is with the thumb and forefinger, one on the round end and one on the sharp end. The other is, with those same fingers, to hold opposite long sides.

To remove a sludge layer from the aura, that is a layer that seems to be very dense and is blocking other flows of subtle energy, you will need to sweep down the body from the top of the head to beyond the feet at the height of the layer. Start at one side and work down the body several times. You may find it easier to change sides once you have reached the centre line. If you feel that the layer is still there, try sweeping from the centre line of the body towards the edge of the body.

Different types of wands can be used in this manner. As it removes the unwanted layer, it seems to leave behind its own energy. A Rose

Quartz wand can provide a gentle removal. An Amethyst wand can take away sludge caused by trauma and replace it with the energy needed to continue and change. If the clogged layer seems to have affected the person's overall energy and enthusiasm, consider using the energetic Citrine.

Once the clearing has taken place, wands can be used to massage the aura. Even if no auric cleansing is needed, a massage with a Rose Quartz, Amethyst or Fluorite wand can be very enjoyable. If the client needs further invigoration, consider using the Citrine. It does not matter if you do not have several different crystal wands; use what you have. Remember to keep your intention clear. Proceed in exactly the same way as you would for the auric clearing. This time work a few inches above the body. When you have finished working down the body, go to the top of the head and stroke down from the brow to the work surface; continue this movement all round the head. Then go to the feet and stroke down from the toes to the heels. You can then return to the torso and stroke from the centre line to the sides. All of these movements are using the wand just off the body.

Wearing crystals

The last part of this unit is a cross between using crystals on and off the body. This is wearing crystals as healing jewellery. Wearing crystals is a very good way of utilising the positive energy that they provide. It is also a good method of using the protective nature of certain crystals. There would seem to be two important aspects to remember: first, that the crystals will need very regular cleansing and, if they are mounted in metal, be careful which cleansing method you use as silver can react with salt and non-precious metals may change; and second, the positioning of the crystal and the length of time that it is worn for. There are several ways that the crystal or crystals can be worn. They can be set as a piece of jewellery, in a noble metal such as silver or gold; they can be drilled and have a thong threaded through them; or they can be placed in a pouch which is worn on a thong or placed in clothing.

The positioning of the crystal can assist in the way in which it works. For those suffering with a sore throat the crystal should be as near to the throat as possible. If the problem is a matter of the heart, try placing the crystal over the Heart Chakra. A heart-shaped Rose Quartz works well. If they are feeling spaced out or ungrounded, try to position the crystal as near to the Base Chakra as possible. Crystals used in jewellery are often of a much higher quality than those found in healing shops. They are, of course, also more expensive. They may be cut to show off the colour and brilliance. These gem-quality stones are normally clearer and their colour stronger than the tumbled stone. This can also make them more potent. This is useful, as they tend to be smaller. It also means that the length of time they are worn for becomes very important.

When using crystals as jewellery do remember that they can be very potent. Do not wear them for days and days or every day. This is particularly important when applied to some of the darker stones such as Obsidian as they may start to make you feel unwell or depressed if left for too long. Remember that a treatment may take 30 minutes and be very effective but you may wear a piece of jewellery all day, which is over 20 times as long. Unless you are trying to learn about a crystal, do not wear the same piece of crystal jewellery all of the time. This applies to other crystals as well. If you have crystals in the room where you sleep then remember to cleanse them and change them regularly.

EXERCISES

The main exercise for this unit is to work with the wand once you have acquired it. Do not worry if you cannot obtain one for a while, just return to this unit when you do. The exercise is to get to know your wand and try the different methods of using them.

Before working with other people, spend some time with your wand. Meditate with it and ask questions on how to use it. This may provide additional information. Then try working on yourself using the wand in different ways. These can include cutting out negative energy, spiralling out negative energy, adding energy, removing sludgy layers from the aura and auric massage.

Then repeat these on people as the opportunity arises. Do not try them all on one person in one session, as the effect may be rather drastic.

UNIT 9 – CRYSTALS AND OTHER THERAPIES

The work we have discussed up to now has been stand-alone crystal healing. Crystals have the benefit of being multi-purpose. They can be used with all sorts of other complementary therapies; in particular, they work very well with some of the physical therapies including reflexology and aromatherapy, as well as other energy therapies like reiki. This unit is intended as general information and as specific information for practitioners of other therapies; so I hope therapists will excuse the repetition of information that is already well known to them.

Reflexology

The first therapy to look at and combine with crystals is reflexology. Reflexology takes as its premise that the body and all of its parts are reflected in the feet and the hands. There are several different types of reflexology; but even so, this basis remains very similar. Crystal can be applied to all types of foot and hand reflexology. It is now widely accepted as an effective treatment for some ailments for some people. To say it will cure everything for everybody would be failing to look at why the person is ill and for how long they have had the complaint, or for how long it has been developing before the symptoms became obvious.

In reflexology, the main work is on the feet. There are several reasons for this, the main one being that the meridians that come through or terminate at the feet pass through or are connected to all the major organs and parts of the body. The meridians that terminate in the hands do not provide such an advantageous coverage of the body. Having stated that, when working on the hands it becomes obvious that they provide their own input to reflexology and in certain cases can provide a more beneficial treatment.

Crystal grids

The normal position for the client in reflexology is either lying down or sitting with the legs and feet supported on a reclining chair or stool. This provides a good environment in which to use crystals. Crystals can be used in reflexology in several ways. The first is around the body in a grid. This can be helpful for those who are suffering from emotional problems such as stress or unhappiness. Using the crystal grids is explained in Unit 8. The crystals are placed around the whole body with stones such as Rose Quartz, Black Tourmaline or a stone such as Turquoise, which has great healing and protective properties. If the couch or chair will not cope with a perfect geometric shape, try placing the crystals at the corners and halfway down the person. Again, before using this system, try it for yourself by lying in the shape that fits into your working area. Try to team up with a reflexologist who has similar ideas and practise using crystals while giving each other treatments.

Crystal layouts

Another way of using crystals is to place a basic layout on the client while undertaking a reflexology treatment. The drawback to this method is that you will have to divide your energy between the crystals, which may need moving during a treatment, and the reflexology where you normally do not lose physical contact with the client. Although it can be effective I suggest that, at this stage, you understand the process, but do not try it unless you feel that it is essential and when you do use it try to monitor the client very carefully.

Crystals around the feet

The easiest way of combining reflexology and crystals is to build layouts around the feet. Trying to keep crystals on the feet can be very difficult unless some method of attaching them is employed, which is not recommended. There are two ways of using crystals around the feet, with the feet on the ground and with the feet raised.

Sometimes after a reflexology treatment, when the client is sitting quietly, crystals can be arranged around the feet. The other way requires an interpretation of the way the feet are positioned so that the toes, which represent the head, are nearest the crystals designed for the head and those that are normally placed on the lower chakras are near the heel. In general, if you look at the feet from the side, if the toes are pointing away from the body, the head is treated as away from the body, that is the other way around to the client and the reverse is true, that when the toes are towards the body, the toes and the head are in the same direction.

Using crystals around the feet during a reflexology treatment provides a great deal of flexibility in the way they are utilised. Very simple supportive layouts can be used; the crystals need only be very small and they do not get in the way. If you are prepared, the stones can be changed during a treatment. Because you are working in a small area, they can be monitored very easily and you do not lose contact with the client. The feet can be scanned as you work.

Scanning the feet

Before applying a single crystal or touching the feet, it is a good idea to scan the feet. You can scan the body before starting the treatment as well. When scanning the feet remember that you are working in a much smaller area than is used for normal crystal healing. This makes the scanning harder, so try to identify where you normally pick up the energy in your hands and make sure that you use that part of your hand. You can also use a single finger; the second finger normally works well.

Another approach is to use a wand on areas of the feet that are painful or where the skin is not suitable for direct manipulation. A wand or a series of wands are ideally suited as precise direction is important when working on such a small area. Where necessary the wand can be used after physical manipulation. This has the benefit of your having a good idea of what is happening within that part of the foot after the physical manipulation.

Foot chakra balance

There are some layouts around the feet that can be applied after the main treatment and then left for ten to 15 minutes. If you provide a reflexology chakra massage and balance at the end of the treatment, try placing a small chakra balance set of stones between the feet. This is the same as the normal chakra balance set of crystals except the stones are much smaller, probably a maximum of one centimetre in all directions. The stones are placed between the feet, not on the body; the order is the same with the Amethyst near the big toes, working down to the Hematite by the heel. With the client already relaxed, if not asleep, the effect can be very advantageous. Although if they are awake and lying down it may be better for the client if they were moved and sitting up in a comfortable chair, as they have already been on their backs for a long time (see Figure 9.1).

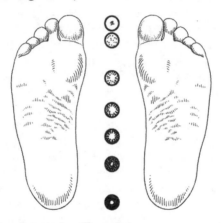

Figure 9.1   Crystal reflexology

Two Clear Quartz crystals

For problems that relate to the bonier parts of the body such as backache or shoulder pains, a pair of Clear Quartz crystals can be used. This process is based on the use of two crystals described earlier in the book. Only small crystals are required, those that are about 2.5 to 3.5 centimetres long seem to work very well. This process involves trying to reduce the energy block that may be causing the physical symptoms and then to assist the energy to flow again. If we assume that the energy flow comes from the head, to the spine and then to the upper and lower limbs, the idea is very simple. By using the crystals as jump-leads the energy flow can be restarted and blockages cleared. To start with, the crystals are used on the feet near the place that represents the area that has the symptoms.

If we take as an example a problem in the shoulder the crystals would be applied as follows: one crystal is held pointing towards the area just above the shoulder reflex, the second crystal is held with the base pointing to just below the shoulder reflex. These are then held until, using intuition, the area feels cleared. There are sometimes physical releases, there may be twitches or pulses in the area that you are working on or along the spine reflex, so keep your attention on the area. Then move the crystals further away, the upper one towards the spine reflex and the lower one towards the elbow reflex. Again, keep them there until you feel that the energy has regained some of its flow. Slowly move each one, the upper towards the spine or head and the lower towards the hand until they are at the head or neck and the hand (see Figure 9.2).

This process works very well after the physical manipulation around the shoulder when the blockages and deposits may have been dislodged.

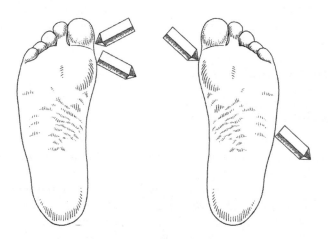

Figure 9.2   Using two Clear Quartz crystals

Other layouts around the feet

For those who are suffering from lack of energy or overload a combination of crystals placed around their feet may help. Many clients who have already had reflexology understand the benefit that the treatment can provide, just in the realms of relaxation. Reflexology clients often say how relaxing the treatment has been, or how they have not felt so relaxed for as long as they can remember. Therefore, it is important to choose the type of crystals with great care so that they complement the relaxation process and do not work against it. This is because the relaxation enables the body to start concentrating on regenerating itself, not just keeping going at all costs. This process is both preventive and curative. Please remember that in this state the client is likely to be open to subtle energy influences, which is why the reflexologist tends to keep in constant physical contact with the client so that they are not coming in and out of their auric fields.

The types of crystals that can be used need to give safety and clarity thus complementing the relaxed state. For those in this normal busy state try a combination of six small Black Tourmaline crystals and six small Blue Beryl (Aquamarine) crystals. The Black Tourmaline provides a security and a protection against other energy fields. It also gives a gentle grounding, a sort of smoothing down. The Aquamarine with its blue colour is a very clear crystal. It provides a calming effect but also helps provide clarity, often in a way that connects to the great source of knowledge. It assists in making the connection to who we are in the greater scheme of things. If you feel that the person needs a little more energy then try Tourmalated Quartz, so that they get the effects of the Black Tourmaline with the energetic response of the Clear Quartz.

These crystals should be placed in two sets of six alternating crystals around the feet. If they are placed a few inches from the feet then there is room for all the hand movements required in the treatment. Other examples include using sets of six small Sodalite stones. These are good for the person who has pushed himself or herself almost too far, as they assist in calming the mind. The Sodalite will work very well with the relaxing effect of the reflexology helping to reduce the anxiety and fear that may have built up with the stress from whatever source. The six crystals are placed around the feet so that there is one near the gap between the two heels and one just below the toes.

For those that are lacking in energy, and perhaps confidence, try a set of Carnelians. These provide a supportive and warming effect. They can be very useful for women who have lost their own being or who are starting out again after bringing up their children. If the client is just run down, mentally and physically, a set of six Jaspers can be of assistance. Green Jasper can provide a calming and strengthening action. It also assists in bringing an overall balance to the body systems. Red Jasper provides stimulation at the basic level. It relates to the lower chakras and because of this can help with grounding, while increasing the motivation of getting going. Again, this works well with reflexology treatments as another aspect of the treatment is that it can, by stimulating the feet, make the connection to the grounding energy stronger.

The intention of this unit is not to be a list of crystals, but by listing the ones that work well with reflexology it provides a guide as to which stones to try on yourself first. The following crystals work well in a six-stone layout: Hematite, Black Tourmaline, Carnelian, Aventurine, Red Jasper, Bloodstone, Green Jasper, Aquamarine, Citrine, Clear Quartz points, Sodalite, Rose Quartz, Blue Lace Agate, Tiger's Eye, Lapis Lazuli, Amazonite, Rhodochrosite and Moonstone. There are, of course, many others, and after trying them out on yourself you will develop your own sets.

Crystals and reiki

Reiki is a gentle but effective hands-on treatment using the channelling of the Universal Energy. In basic reiki, the hands are placed on the body in a series of set movements and, depending on the individual acting as the reiki channeller, moved when they feel a subtle change in the energy or after a preset period if nothing is felt. The addition of crystals to a reiki session seems to work very well. The basic reiki treatment works through the seven main chakras together with parts of the subtle energy body. Therefore, if the client is lying down, a simple chakra layout works well using the basic set of crystals in the normal places.

As the treatment progresses, the stones can be monitored and removed when necessary. The client has to turn over halfway through the treatment session so they need to be removed before then. This provides the opportunity of placing a chakra balance set of crystals on the back. These are placed in similar positions to the front with the Crown and Base Chakras off the body; the Brow Chakra on the back of the head or next to the back of the head if the head is turned to one side; the Throat Chakra stone is placed on the back of the neck and the others down the spine (see Unit 10). The crystals should be a cleansed set and not the ones taken off the front of the body.

A grid of crystals can also be placed around the working area. Some people practise reiki with the client sat in an upright chair, crystals can be placed around the bottom of the chair or even taped underneath if the practitioner is worried about standing on them as they walk around. There are many crystals that work well in this position including Rose Quartz, Aventurine, Clear Quartz and Amethyst. Reiki also blends well with a cluster or lump of crystal placed under the workbench or chair.

For those giving treatments to clients who are lying down, a grid can be placed around them. This can be from one of the Sacred Geometry shapes or one crystal at each corner of the couch or even some combination of the two. The crystals used can be based on the requirements of the client and the reasons why they have come for a treatment. If you feel they need further balancing then try using pieces of Aventurine at each corner of the table. If they have a physical problem, then terminated Clear Quartz or Smoky Quartz can be placed pointing out from the corners. It is important to monitor the effect that the crystals are having on the client and to remove them and replace them with others as you work. After using Clear Quartz or Smoky Quartz you may want to replace it with Clear Quartz pointing inwards or Rose Quartz as a gentle healing and caring stone or with Citrine points to provide a renewal of energy for the individual.

Reiki can also be used to cleanse the crystals, either during a treatment or afterwards. The best way of doing this is, while using the appropriate symbols, ask the reiki masters to cleanse away the negative energy that has accumulated in the crystals and to replace it with positive energy. This leaves the crystals ready for use. You have to gauge whether this is sufficient cleansing and whether the stones need a deeper cleansing. In most cases the reiki cleansing should be sufficient.

Aromatherapy and crystals

Using crystals with aromatherapy is, in some respects, different from the other treatments. It is important to try the ideas before applying them to clients. It is hard to place crystals on the body during a massage session and because of the movement of the limbs and body during a session, placing crystals on a couch is not a practical answer. Crystals can be placed in the room, or underneath the couch. Crystals placed in a healing room always add to the treatment in some way. The important factor is to make sure they are cleansed regularly. If the session has been a very heavy one then the cleansing should be undertaken before the next treatment, even leaving the crystals in the room could be detrimental to the next client and possibly the therapist.

Perhaps the best way to combine aromatherapy and crystals is by using the crystals to enhance the properties of the oils. Either placing crystals in the oil or very close to the bottle can achieve this. A general way of doing this would be to crystal enhance the carrier oil by placing a crystal in the oil container before it is used. Several bottles of carrier oil could be prepared with different crystals and the appropriate one or even a mix of two used when preparing the working oil. This process is similar to the preparation of gem elixirs, which are fluids, normally water, or alcohol, that have had crystals placed in them. The major difference is that gem elixirs often use sunlight to activate the mixture. The oils used in aromatherapy tend to react badly to sunlight, so the steeping of crystals in oils should be undertaken in darkness or dark containers.

You may have to experiment to find the right length of time to steep the crystals or to place the crystals around the bottle. If you place the crystals around the bottle, try using a Sacred Geometric shape such as the six-pointed star to increase the vibrational energy and pointing terminated crystals towards the bottle. Try leaving the oil and crystals for 24 hours and then test the oil. Then try for a shorter or longer period depending on your results. The basic crystals make good additions and for special cases, very specific oils can be made up using an appropriate oil and crystal.

Other treatments

Crystals make a good addition to all treatments and healing rooms. They can enhance the work and add to the general atmosphere of the room. Again, the emphasis must be placed on keeping the crystals clean and energised. There are very few things that are worse than a treatment room or even a waiting room that has dirty, worn-out crystals. Clients who are undertaking other forms of therapy, particularly where there is a lot of emotional release taking place, can hold crystals. This can provide them with additional support. In these situations, Rose Quartz works really well. If the situation is to do with loss, then try Amethyst crystals. The client can hold one crystal in each hand.

EXERCISES

As this unit is specialised there are no general exercises. If you wish to incorporate crystals into your other work, make sure you have worked through the rest of the book and in particular worked with the crystals on yourself, both with just crystals and then using them within the treatment you are undertaking. With reflexology try placing the crystals around your feet and using the chakra balance to gain an understanding of the change in feelings that can occur. With reiki, use crystals during self-treatment sessions. Place a chakra balance set on yourself before starting the self-treatment. Then try grids and other patterns of crystals off the body during self-treatment sessions. Remember to record all your findings so that you can refer back to them. Undertake as many trials as you can.

With aromatherapy, try making Crystal-enhanced oils, and comparing them with ordinary oils. If you use sitting with or meditating with the oils to help understand their properties, do the same with the oils that have been enhanced with the crystals. Do this for all of the oils you have made up. If you feel that a particular oil and a particular crystal would make a good combination, try it and see if your intuition was correct.

UNIT 10 - DIFFERENT CRYSTAL LAYOUTS

This unit looks at different forms of crystal layout. In earlier units, we have looked at some preset layouts and at developing your own layouts depending on the need of the client. As has been mentioned the chakras are not confined to the front of the body. They are also on the back of the body. It is also possible that the chakras are complete bands around the body, approachable from all directions. This is because they are feeding the subtle energy mechanism within the body and connecting up to the auras, meridians, nervous system and other energy paths throughout the body. The energy that is approached from the front seems to be slightly different from that at the back. An example of this is the feelings that we get when approached from behind by a person, whether they are known to us or not. The feeling we perceive is different to the feeling we get when approached from the front.

Front and back scanning

To understand this further, try feeling the energy from both the back and the front of a person and comparing the two. The easiest way to do this is with them standing up so that you can easily access both the back and the front. As before, you can use your hands and your pendulum. Start with your hands: prepare yourself in the normal way by grounding and asking your helpers for assistance. If you are worried about your client having to stand, sit them on a stool or sideways on an upright chair so that their front and back are both accessible. As you work, note down your findings. Start with the front of the body working down from the head. Allow your intuition to work with you by keeping your mind as clear as possible. Try to treat the exercise like a meditation, let the information flow into your hands.

As you feel over each chakra, concentrate on that chakra alone, with your hand at about three or four inches away from the body. If you need to, move your hand nearer or further away from the body to see if there is any change in the sensation that you perceive. In addition, by moving your hand, you are cutting through the energy layers, which may cause greater feeling in your hand. Continue this exercise until you have reached the feet. Start again, this time feeling over the back of the body. Take your time; use both hands if you wish. Concentrate over the chakra points, if you are not sure where they are use your hands to try to identify their location. Note down your findings and compare them with the front of the body. What differences did you find and what do you think that this implies?

Front and back with a pendulum

Next, try the same exercise using your pendulum. If you are unsure about taking readings from a person in a vertical position, there are two ways that it can be achieved. The first is to take the reading from where the weight of the pendulum is, the second is to place the pendulum in your sending hand and to use your receiving hand to move over the body in the same way as normal scanning, except move slowly to allow the information to be interpreted by the pendulum. In both cases, ask the pendulum questions, such as to indicate where the chakra is, about the chakra or to indicate the energy flow in the chakra. Start on the front at the top and work down covering as much of the body as possible. Then work on the back and compare your findings to those you obtained for the front. As always, there is never a simple answer. It is possible that the front and the back give the same results. It is also possible that you get different results. One great benefit is that it may highlight an area that is in need of intensive work. This will be apparent if one particular chakra gives a reading showing blockage or closure on both the back and the front. Remember that the Crown and Base Chakra should give the same reading, as they are the same chakra whether the reading is taken from the front or the back.

If you get different readings from back and front let your intuition loose to see whether you can find out why. The basic survival from the Base Chakra and the spiritual connection at the Crown Chakra are provided by the single chakras of base and crown. It is the other five that have a difference in energy between the front and back. The energy from the front of the chakras seems to be related to the everyday necessities and the ability of the individual to maintain them. The energy from the rear entry points of the chakras seems to be at a higher level and relate more to the emotional and spiritual nature of the individual. There is, of course, an overlap between the front and back chakras, but reasonable results when scanning the front entry points of the chakras may be hiding deeper emotional problems that may only show on the rear entry points. Having separated the energy forms it must be stressed that ordinarily the front chakra scan provides sufficient information for normal treatments.

In some senses, working with the subtle energy of people is like looking at a three-dimensional picture of them which has more than three dimensions. It is like trying to gauge the depth of a hole when looking at a photograph taken from directly above without lights and possibly with your eyes shut! Although there is new knowledge being uncovered all the time, we have a long way to go to understand and utilise the natural forces that we have.

Having scanned the rear chakras, you can apply a crystal layout. Normally a layout would be applied to the front first then, after repeating the scan, a layout applied to the back with the client lying on their front.

Energy leaks

When working with these energies also check the knees, feet, elbows and hands. Get the client to lift their arms and scan down the sides of the body. This may identify places where there are energy leaks that are not clearly discernible from the front or the back. Energy leaks are where subtle energy, which can be part of the person's life force, is not held within the body and for some reason escapes. There can be many reasons why this happens including previous or current illness, environmental situations including underground energy lines (black lines, lay lines, water courses or mineral deposits), or even due to the absence of parts of the soul caused by fear and trauma. The leak may also be through several layers of the aura, so it is important to both check a leak and to start working on the repair as far away from the body as possible.

If you find an energy leak it is sometimes possible to perceive it either visually or mentally and it can look like a firework with sparks flying out from the end, or like an oozing mess leaking out slowly. The first thing to consider is why is this happening; it may require more than just crystals to stop the leak. If it has been caused by trauma, an accident or abuse, specialist work from an expert in retrieval may be needed. Do not attempt any work at this level unless you are competent and confident to do so. If the leak is caused by any other reason then you can try sealing the leak with crystals. This can be done in many ways, although it may depend on the way the leak is occurring, and the only way to find out what works is to try various methods.

Repairing energy leaks

The first is the simple spiralling Clear Quartz crystal. Working around the leak area, with the termination pointed towards the client, and about 30 centimetres away (more if you feel it is necessary), slowly rotate your hand holding the crystal pointing towards the leak in a clockwise direction, while moving inwards thus forming a spiral around the leak. Continue with this until you reach the body, by which time your circular motion will be very small. As you do this, imagine your moving crystal is creating a cover over the leak so that it cannot escape. Next using an appropriate crystal wand, such as Rose Quartz, and using one of the flat sides, massage all over the body taking extra time over the area of the leak, using the domed end to seal the area. When you have finished, check the area with your vision, inner sight, hand and pendulum to make sure the leak has stopped. Repeat once more in this session if the leak persists. It is important to see the person again after a week to ensure that the seal has worked and that the leak has not sprung from elsewhere.

If the leak has started again by the next session, but is not as serious, repeat the sealing with the Clear Quartz crystal and massage. Before doing this try to find out from the client, without putting the idea into their minds, whether they have had more energy, enthusiasm or other positive feelings after the previous treatment. They may tell you this without any prompting. If they do not, check them very carefully to see whether the leak has moved. If it has, repeat the process or try an alternative method. Try to discover what is causing the leak, as it can be for many reasons including stress, previous injury or physical trauma.

Working with oozy slow-moving leaks is different. To seal the leak it is sometimes necessary to try to remove the oozing substance before sealing the hole. To do this use your Clear Quartz terminated crystal or wand to hook out the thick energy. Once hooked shake it carefully to the earth, asking it to be transmuted to positive energy for the good of all. Then, when you feel all this energy has been cleared, seal the area with the spiral movement and finish with a crystal massage.

A third way of working, which will be covered later in the unit, is to use a locally placed grid of crystals. This is when the grid is placed around the leak, rather than around the person. Use applicable crystals; the Clear Quartz can be very effective. Place them with the points facing in towards the leak, and if you feel it will help, hold an additional crystal above the leak. Visualise the energy stopping the leak. If the client is aware of what is happening, get them to visualise the leak closing and their energy improving. Client visualisation can be used throughout crystal healing work. An alternative method is to place the Clear Quartz crystals in this same manner and to place another crystal behind each one. A Rose Quartz or Aventurine can be of great assistance. Finish off with a crystal massage and check to ensure that the leak has subsided.

Multiple crystals at each chakra

Returning to layouts, the next part deals with the use of more than one crystal and more than one type of crystal at each chakra. This is used when you want to give more than one type of crystal energy to a particular chakra or part of the body. This can be applied in two basic ways, the first is to use more than one crystal of the same type, bringing in additional energy; and second, using a combination of crystals. The first is a localised version of using crystal grids. This can be used when you feel that direct application of a single crystal will not give you the result you are looking for. As an example, when working on the Heart Chakra, you may want to surround it with Rose Quartz rather than just placing a single stone over the chakra. This appears to provide more of a supportive feeling, and although the action is not quite so direct, it can produce a stronger feeling of support. You can continue to place a larger grid around the whole person as well, which will add to the overall effect of the healing session.

Localised grids

The number of stones you use is up to you. It depends on what you have available. You could use just two. These two can be placed either side of the Heart Chakra; or one above and one below, which then helps to connect the Heart Chakra to the Thymus and Throat Chakras above and to the Solar Plexus below, with a gentle caring link. This can be expanded to four crystals, with one each side and one above and one below. A six-sided star can also be created, with one crystal above, one below and two equally spaced on each side (see Figure 10.1).

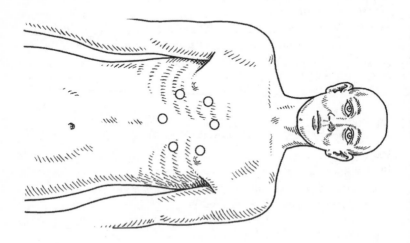

Figure 10.1   Heart grid

This approach can also be used when trying to remove negative or unwanted energy from the chakra. In this case, six Clear Quartz, Smoky Quartz or Amethyst crystals can be used. These need not be large; sizes of one centimetre in length can be very effective. Place these in a six-pointed star around the chakra with the terminations pointing out, with two points on the centre line, and two on each side. Check on this layout to see when the work is complete, you may want to charge the area with Clear Quartz or some other crystal. If you use Clear Quartz, either use another set of crystals or cleanse the stones before reapplying them. On replacing the stones, put them in the same pattern, but this time with the terminations pointing in towards the centre. To protect the chakras above and below the crystal grid during the removal stage you may want to place a Clear Quartz crystal pointing towards the grid in front of each one to stop the negative energy being reabsorbed.

In general, this is a way of working on individual chakras. There may also be occasions when you want to apply the idea to specific parts of the body. This is fine. Locate the place that needs to be worked upon and build the grid around it. If it is on an extremity of the body, construct the grid on the ground or table around the part of the body requiring treatment. If the first part is to clear the area, use the crystals pointing away from the centre, and when you want to fill the area with positive energy either use tumbled stones in the grid or Clear Quartz with terminations towards the centre, or both.

Combining crystals

The idea of using a combination of crystals in one area has been referred to several times. We will now look at this in greater depth although most of the groundwork required has already been discussed. There are really two main factors to consider. The first is the crystals and their relationship to each other and the second is the pattern of the layout used. If you use a combination of crystals, and unless the situation is very strange, the crystals should be working in harmony with each other. They need not be the same colour, but the effect each type of crystal produces should resonate with other stones in the layout. If they did not resonate, it would be like producing incorrect notes when playing an instrument in an orchestra. Normally, individual notes resonate to create a melodic sound. Play an incorrect note in the orchestra and the whole sound will appear incorrect. The same will happen with two types of crystal that are not in harmony; they will produce a discordant result.

It is important to choose crystals that work well together. First, why do you want to use more than one type of crystal? Normally to enhance the effect of a particular crystal or to provide a more rounded treatment and increase the efficacy of the treatment. Different crystals can be used when you do not have enough of one particular type. To select your different crystals use your knowledge of the properties of the crystals and if necessary meditate with two you have selected and ask if and then how they will work together. Another option is to use your pendulum and dowse over the various crystals and ask if they will work well together.

Having made your selection, where and in what pattern are they then placed? This partly depends on how many of each crystal you have available as well as the reason for working in that area. If you were working on the Heart Chakra, one simple combination would be Rose Quartz and Amazonite. Amazonite is a greeny blue stone that can assist in calming the emotions. The combination works well when there is a great deal of anguish that is restricting the release of the cause of the emotional upset. The Amazonite helps to calm the emotional upset, while the Rose Quartz provides love and emotional support. Then the upset may be vocalised. If you have four of each stone build a grid around the Heart Chakra with alternating stones.

Another example would be at the Brow Chakra. A simple layout of a single Sodalite with a piece of Aquamarine on either side can be very calming and clearing. Each stone needs to be very small, between 0.5 and one centimetre. The Sodalite is a very calming stone and can help to decrease the internal chatter that takes place in the mind and the Aquamarine is calming with the ability to add clarity of vision, helping to open up an individual's innate intuitive abilities. An alternative process with these two stones would be to calm the mind first with the Sodalite then replace it with the Aquamarine to open up the light.

There are many different combinations of crystals that you can devise, test and use. You may well find that you develop your own favourites that you like to work with. Sometimes each person who comes to see you has a very similar problem, and you use the same set repeatedly for a week or longer. This seems to be normal.

Too many crystals

One important factor is not to have too many crystals in any one layout. Remember that the idea of crystal healing is to assist individuals to heal themselves. To bring the body, mind, emotions and spirit back into balance. A set of several stones around each chakra plus layouts around the body may not be as effective as a simple layout that concentrates on one particular concern, with the rest of the layout acting as a balance for the whole body. The different influences caused by a large number of crystals may be confusing to the body's energy system. It is as if we try to do everything at once, rarely does it work, with a result that nothing is done. Several relatively simple layouts spread over a period may be much more effective than one giant pile of crystals in one session.

Single crystal type layouts

The next set of layouts to look at are enormous in number, almost as many layouts as there are crystals types available. This is because this section is about single crystal type layouts. That is the use of only one type of crystal in some form of layout. That layout can be on the whole body or just surrounding one part or chakra. Some stones are more suited to this type of work than others. The more general stones are a good starting point, with some of the unusual ones being suitable for specialised purposes. One of the nicest and most loving layouts comes within this section: the Rose Quartz layout. This is like being wrapped in cotton wool with exotic oils and any other caring fantasy you wish to imagine.

Advanced Rose Quartz layout

Do try this one on yourself, especially when you are not feeling in the best way towards the world or other people. The basic layout, which can be modified according to need, is a Rose Quartz crystal at each of the seven main chakras, plus one or two at the feet and one in each hand. If you have enough crystals, make a simple Rose Quartz grid around where you are going to work. Make sure you are comfortable and will not be disturbed. This is a good layout to do just before going to sleep, because you do not have to come out from it in any sudden manner. It is a good idea to use smooth crystals rather than natural crystals in case you roll over and end up lying on them. This is the basic layout; you can alter it by using the crystals in different places to provide the best treatment possible.

For clients that have come for a treatment as a matter of course, rather than for specific reasons this can be a good all-round caring and preventive treatment. It is preventive because the energy from Rose Quartz is of Universal Love and care, and this feeling relaxes the body, mind and spirit thus enabling it to be better at stopping the influx of illness. So, if you can manage a self-treatment once a week, see whether there is any change in your overall health pattern. Of course, the healer is always the last one to have a treatment, so try very hard to give yourself that pleasure.

This general format can be used with many types of crystal with minor modifications. In a sense, it is the opposite of using more than one type of crystal in one place. This takes the energy of a particular crystal and applies it to all of the person. Another way of working with a single type of crystal is to build a grid around the outside of the person, this time without applying any other crystals. This gives a different sensation of being enveloped within the crystal energy. As an experiment, try alternating the single crystal type grid layout and the single crystal type chakra layout without a grid, to identify the difference. A derivative of these layouts is to use a simple layout around one part of the person or a chakra with a single type of crystal.

The effect of single crystal work can be very exciting. The crystals do not need to be large as small ones seem to work very effectively. These types of layouts can be helpful for specific problems, either where they have reached a chronic stage and the work needs to be symptomatic for the first stages of treatment or where a problem is causing pain or annoyance, and although it is important to view treatments holistically it is sometimes better to deal with the symptoms directly. A treatment can start with a small single type grid around a troublesome area, possibly a Clear or Smoky Quartz clearing grid. This is then removed and further stones are added later in the treatment to assist in the balancing of the individual.

With all of these treatments it is important to remain as flexible as possible. If you see or feel a change in the person and the crystals use that as a signal to remove, change or leave the crystals alone; which you do depends on the situation. Remove or change them if the energy has altered; leave them alone if there is still more change to come. Also listen to your intuition; the signal may be to stop just there and allow the person time to assimilate the changes that have taken place and are still to occur within them. Sometimes it is very easy to try to fix everything at once. However, sometimes a little bit at a time can be far more effective than one big attempt. Another word of warning: if the client needs to be invigorated or is very lethargic do not try to increase their energy too quickly; it is better to take it slowly. A few crystals will be very effective even if you feel as if you should put them in a room filled with Citrine or Clear Quartz to get them going. Their system will only change at the speed it can change at; overloading the process will not be of benefit.

EXERCISES

Many areas have been covered in this unit, all of which need to be tried and practiced before application. Remember that if you are using a new stone, meditate with it and learn its properties by living with it before using it on other people.

The first exercise is to get used to scanning the back as well as the front. If possible, practice this on someone who does not mind having to stand for a while as this gives you the best opportunity to move around and compare the energies back and front. Feel the front, then the back and immediately compare with the front again. Keep trying to notice the subtle differences and listen to your intuition. Note down what you find, ask the person questions that are relevant to what you find to assist you in increasing your skills. Try this as often as you can to build up your knowledge of different energies of different people.

Next, try different combination of crystals. One way to do this is to undertake your normal process of finding the powers of stones. First, choose the two crystals you want to try together, and then meditate with each individual stone. Next, meditate with the two stones together and ask about the synergistic energy that they develop. You can also ask about the possible way of placing the crystals on the body. The final stage is to try these out on yourself to feel the effect that they have. Depending on the crystals place them around or on a relevant chakra and spend time with them. Repeat this exercise with as many combinations as you wish to try.

Having worked with different stones it is now time to work with several of the same crystal. The first exercise is to place yourself in a grid of Rose Quartz. Prepare your space and then place the Rose Quartz in a six-pointed star grid, with one above your head and one below your feet and two on each side. An alternative is to sit cross-legged or on a meditation stool in the middle of the grid. Spend as long as you can in this or as stated in the text try it where you sleep so that the feeling can allow you to relax into sleep. Try this with other crystals, but do not try sleeping in a grid with other stones if they are too vibrant or you may not sleep!

Using sets of the same stones, try them on relevant chakras or other parts of yourself that need healing. Then try them on someone who may be able to feed back information. Use different crystals when you feel that they may be needed. Do not just place them on individuals because you want to find out what happens.

UNIT 11 – CRYSTALS AROUND THE HOUSE

In this unit, the crystal is taken out of the treatment room and we look at how to use the powers of crystals in different ways. Crystals can be beneficial in most situations, in the home, in the office, on the move, and even when applied to other aspects of our lives, such as in astrology, in feng shui and when converted into another form of healing tool.

Sacred space

The first consideration is one of the aspects looked at the beginning of the book, that of sacred space. By now, sacred space may have become part of your everyday existence. When crystals are taken out of the healing area, it is nice both to create sacred space for them and for them to help create sacred space. This is, of course, a puzzle, but with careful work, a result of the crystal in a sacred space can be achieved. To recap, sacred space is a special place or area that has been prepared to assist you achieve a slightly different level of consciousness. It was used in the preparation of the healing area and for the meditation place where you have gained knowledge about your crystals. It can also be used to create special places anywhere, in the home, office or when travelling. The idea is that the sacred space is somewhere special, and that somewhere can even be you and your immediate surroundings. By placing a crystal within a room, in a particular place, that place becomes a special place, a sacred space, because of the energy that the crystal imparts. It is also good to have prepared the space into which the crystal is placed by removing physical dirt and clutter and by smudging or burning essential oils such as juniper or grapefruit in a diffuser.

To create sacred space in your home is not difficult. Placing crystals in your home is not too difficult either. The question that has to be answered is probably what crystals to place where. The best way to decide this is by intuition. You are the one who can sense what each room or space requires, you know what each room is used for and by whom. Before placing the crystal you have chosen, sit and meditate with the crystal and ask whether it will take on the task you are asking it to do. Explain why you have chosen it and what you hope may be achieved by having it available. If you get a strong feeling that this is not the right crystal, or this is not the correct place for that crystal, repeat the meditation with another crystal or at another place until you feel that the crystal, space and purpose are suited.

Crystals in the house

Next, prepare the place. To do this physically clean and tidy the area where you are going to place your crystal. Smudge the area to clear it of any negative energy and finally place your crystal in the prepared area. You may want to add a candle, a vase of flowers, a special photograph or image and later other crystals. Crystals can be used in the home for many reasons. Different sorts of crystals can be used in different rooms. In rooms where inspiration and the will to keep at work is required energising stones such as Citrine or Carnelian can be used, these can be helpful in the kitchen where meals are prepared when everyone is low on energy. If there is a room where a lot of mental work is taking place, an area where people are studying, then consider Fluorite, Lapis Lazuli or Aquamarine as these assist the mind and can help with the connection to the universe. Clear Quartz will also work in these situations.

If the rooms are for peaceful activities or for sleeping in, then crystals like Rose Quartz, Amethyst and Blue or Green Calcite can be very helpful. A grid of Rose Quartz around the bed can assist in the loving process, both of yourself and others, and it may help you or others let go of the stresses and strains of the day. Where there is a feeling of being in an area of negative energy, pieces of Black Tourmaline by the bed may help with protecting the occupants from such energies during the night. If worries keep you awake at night, try a piece of Sodalite by the bed or even under the pillow. This is a very good stone for calming the mind and understanding emotional strangleholds.

Although you can never have too many crystals, sometimes too many different types of crystals may be confusing, particularly where they have diverse energies. Large terminated Clear Quartz or Citrine near a sleeping area will not assist the promotion of a peaceful night. In the same way pieces of Sodalite in a kitchen would not be a good idea as it can produce a sleepy feeling, not what you want where there are machines and sharp tools.

Crystals and plants

Another use of crystals is with plants. A plant that needs love and attention may benefit from a piece of Rose Quartz close by. Clear Quartz will help plants that need to grow and expand. These stones can either be placed in the soil of the flowerpot or on the surface of the soil. Aventurine on the surface of the soil can bring balance to the plant, as houseplants are rarely grown in ideal situations, their growth is often out of balance in terms of roots, foliage and flowers. The green of the Aventurine also looks nice on top of the soil and the stone is not disturbing to people in the room.

Negative energy in buildings

If there are areas in the house that seem to have a negative feel about them, crystals can be used to assist in either moving the negative energy away or in keeping it at bay. Examples of this type of negative energy include somewhere that just does not feel right, a place where accidents happen without any real reason or a bed where the incumbent is often ill. It is possible that these areas exist because of external influences caused by underground and overground natural energy sources, such as water and ore deposits, or even where a serious traumatic event has taken place. There are energy grids above ground and where these cross or coincide with each other, they can produce a negative energy field. It can also be caused by created energy sources including radio waves, electricity supplies and transformers. By using a combination of crystals, it is sometimes possible to move the negative energy away to a place where it will not cause such disruption. How it is moved, or whether it can be moved depends on what is causing it. In general, reasonably sized Clear Quartz points will assist. First, use lots of smudge to start the clearing process. If the energy is in a line or has an edge to it then set up a row of points facing the energy line and visualise the line moving out of the room to a place where it will not cause any harm, at the same time using a wand or large crystal to sweep the energy away. As you see the energy line or edge moving, you may need to move the crystals to keep up the pressure.

After it has moved, cleanse the area with smudge, sound or both, as this helps to remove any lingering negative energy. Also, set up a row of alternating Clear Quartz and Rose Quartz at the edge of the room to stop the negative energy moving back. Place a Rose Quartz in each corner of the room to help keep it feeling friendlier. Aventurine also works well in this situation, alternated with the Rose Quartz, because of its balancing nature. The stones used in this work will need to be very carefully cleansed and replaced regularly; and the work repeated at regular intervals.

Remember that the crystals used in the home will need regular cleansing. They often attract dust, so regular washing as well as smudging will help keep them looking nice and working to their best ability. Keep small or sharp crystals out of reach of small hands and mouths. Children can be very attracted to crystals and some of them do look like sweets but do not taste as nice.

The workplace and crystals

The office or work area is another good place to utilise the benefits of crystals. If you regularly have to deal with people, try placing a protective stone nearby or wear them as part of your daily routine. Crystals such as Black Tourmaline, Turquoise or Amber can assist in providing protection from other people's psychic forces. This works with co-workers as well as clients and customers. If you are in an area that has computer displays or televisions, try placing crystals near them to help reduce the effects of the electromagnetic emissions. Clear Quartz is the greatest of transformers and transducers and can work well near equipment that gives off electromagnetic forces. Another beautiful crystal that helps in this situation is Fluorite, which helps to absorb the energy.

Fluorite comes in many colours and in three basic forms, all of which absorb energy. Fluorite has wonderful crystals, octahedrons that come in many sizes; clusters of tiny octahedron crystals; and massives. Great care must be taken with Fluorite, as it is very soft and prone to physical damage. However, the softness and feel of the crystal is all part of its strength and charm. It is also carved into all sorts of shapes, so if you have a favourite animal or power animal you can consider obtaining one to place near your workstation. As well as providing help in absorbing emissions the Fluorite crystal can also assist the mind and helps to keep your thoughts on the tasks in hand. The stone absorbs so much energy, and even though it does transmute the energy, very regular cleansing is required if the crystals are to continue being effective. Other crystals can be used around computers including Amethyst, Rose Quartz and Tourmaline.

If you work with people in the caring professions, you may find Rose Quartz of use and again it is a protective stone so that you do not absorb other people's negative energy. We are normally taught how to deal with verbal negativity and pain, but rarely with the psychic negativity that is often released at the same time. There are other ways of coping with such problems including straightforward showering, using certain essential oils and meditative practises. However, a few crystals in your pocket or on the desk can help. Crystals on the desk can also create a small diversion, giving you an opportunity to tune into those you are working with.

This list can be extended to most work forms. You may not want to display your interest in crystals so blatantly to your work colleagues, or there may not be room for them, so a small bag of crystals in a locker can also be of help. The wearing of crystals for protection is discussed in the next section. So try using crystals at work, either openly or covertly and see what difference they make.

Amulets and travel bags

If you cannot place crystals in your workspace, or for when you are on the move, even going to the shops, consider making a travel bag or an amulet. An amulet is a device designed to protect you against unwanted forces. These are normally worn close to the body, but they can be carried in a bag such as a purse or briefcase. The amulet can be as simple as a single crystal or more complex as a group of crystals working together both to protect and assist you in your everyday living. You will need small crystals, otherwise, it all gets too heavy to carry comfortably; and tumbled stones work well as the crystals are knocked about and do fall into each other.

The type of bag depends on whether you want to wear it or place it in your purse or bag. An alternative option for wearing crystals is to use drilled crystals on a thong or cord, but please ask the crystals if they want to be drilled. If you buy pre-drilled crystals, they may need a lot of cleansing before they recuperate from the drilling. The bag can be made from almost anything although natural materials must be preferred; artificial materials may set a static electricity problem. Natural fibres allow the energy of the crystals to go where they are needed. Some people like to use small leather pouches; if this is your choice, a small ceremony to thank the animal for the skin is a nice appreciation.

After you have chosen the crystals for your amulet, they need to be specially cleansed and charged for being in an amulet. After charging, you may wish to meditate with them, holding the intention of their purpose in your mind. Remember that they will be in the dark for a long time. Sit and meditate with them and try to appreciate the overall effect that they have. Is this the feeling that you want to create? You may want to remove one or add another. Repeat this process until you are happy with the result. Place the stones in the pouch and put it where it needs to be. If you want to make a selection for other people, the process is the same except you need to visualise the person and their situation when selecting the stones. If the bag is for a special reason, then think of that at the same time as the person.

For a general protective amulet, crystals such as Amber, Black Tourmaline and Turquoise can be combined. If the occasion is a funeral or other function of loss, try including Amethyst, Rose Quartz and Mahogany Obsidian. For exams or other situations where there is a large mental element include good mental stimulators such as Fluorite and Aquamarine. If the crystal bag is needed for times when you are going into crowds or places where a lot of exuberant energy is likely to fly around, such as bars, sales or football matches, use the protective stones and possibly a good grounding stone such as Hematite.

If you are wearing your amulet, you can always place your hand on it to remind yourself of the powers it contains. Amulets or single stones can be placed in your car or on your bike to help keep you alert or even to help keep your car running. I have travelled a long way with a crystal on the dashboard keeping the engine working or the battery charged! Depending on how much use they have you will need to cleanse them regularly. Also, when the crystals in your amulet bag are not in use remember to bring them back out into the light. It is easy to put them in your bag and forget all about them.

Although amulets can be very powerful, it is not a good idea to use them to undertake actions that may be dangerous. For instance, if you are tired, and should not be driving, do not rely on them to keep you awake. In this case, do not drive.

Astrology and birthstones

Crystals are also associated with astrology and birth signs. Each zodiac sign has several crystals associated with it, as has each calendar month. Some people say that you should wear your birth or astrological stone to assist in keeping the zodiac energies; an alternative is that you should use the stone that relates to the zodiac period we are actually in. This is a personal matter and depends on how you view the powers and meaning of astrology. One thought is that when you are working with issues that relate to your astrological sign have one of your zodiac crystals close by. Another is when working through the month and planning or dealing with issues that arise to have the calendar month stone close by. If you feel it is important, you can place your zodiac stone in your amulet crystal bag.

There are crystals associated with many of the astrological functions including all of the planets and elements. As you work through astrological issues each month, it is possible to meditate with the stones that relate to your zodiac sign and the calendar month to assist you on your path. A complete amulet can be made relating to the astrological forces that inhabit your astrological chart.

Table 11.1 contains a list of the most common zodiac stones, Table 11.2 the most common planetary and Table 11.3 the most common month stones. There is a large selection of stones for each zodiac sign, planet and month and the same crystal may be used for more than one. Different lists provide completely different stones.

Aquarius	Hawk's Eye, Turquoise, Agate, Aquamarine
Pisces	Amethyst, Chrysoprase, Tourmaline
Aries	Red Jasper, Carnelian, Bloodstone
Taurus	Carnelian, Rose Quartz, Pin Tourmaline, Emerald, Topaz
Gemini	Citrine, Tiger's Eye, Agate, Chrysocolla, Green Tourmaline
Cancer	Aventurine, Emerald, Rhodochrosite, Moss Agate
Leo	Garnet, Tiger's Eye, Amber, Peridot
Virgo	Citrine, Carnelian, Amazonite, Rose Quartz
Libra	Aquamarine, Smoky Quartz. Aventuringe, Peridot
Scorpio	Carnelian, Obsidian, Moonstone, Garnet
Sagittarius	Amethyst, Sodalite, Turquoise
Capricorn	Amethyst, Peridot, Ruby, Garnet

Table 11.1 Stones of the zodiac

Sun	Diamond, Tiger's Eye
Moon	Moonstone, Pearl, Aquamarine
Mars	Garnet, Ruby
Mercury	Citrine, Topaz
Jupiter	Amethyst, Lapis Lazuli, Sapphire
Saturn	Aquamarine
Venus	Rose Quartz

Table 11.2 Stones of the planets

Crystal Essences

The final part of this unit is the preparation of crystal essences. During the last few decades, there has been a growth in the use of essences, from the Bach Flower Remedies through to reiki essences and, slowly, the crystal essences. Crystal essences are the

January	Garnet
February	Amethyst
March	Aquamarine
April	Diamond
May	Emerald
June	Pearl
July	Ruby
August	Peridot
September	Sapphire
October	Opal
November	Topaz
December	Turquoise

Table 11.3 Stones of the month

energy of the crystal, its essence, placed in a liquid. There are two versions of essences, one where alcohol has been used as the solvent and the other where water is used. In general, the use of water as the essence carrier seems to be satisfactory as far as crystals are concerned. There is no actual process of dissolving the crystal; it is purely the energy of the crystal that is taken into the fluid, in this case into the water.

Different types of water can be used. It needs to be clean and as free from chemicals as possible and full of life as pure water should be. This is one case where recycling is not good. Water from the tap has in most cases lost the life force that it originally had, either because it has been treated several times in a circular route from water company to consumer and back again, or because the treatment to make the water drinkable and additives to keep it safe, destroy the natural energy of water. A good source is natural water that has come from old sources deep underground and holy wells where the water is recognised as having vitality. Well water has normally been filtered through the ground and depending where the water comes from is normally relatively additive free.

Having found a suitable source of water the next stage is to instil the crystal energy into the water. This is normally achieved by the use of direct contact with a catalyst of an additional energy such as sunlight or moonlight. There are exceptions. As we have already seen some crystals are not that fond of water, in which case the crystal and the water need to be placed very close to each other, possibly with a protective grid around them.

An important factor to remember when undertaking the creation of crystal essences, or for that matter any essences, is the effect of other energy sources nearby. Other energy sources include electromagnetic emissions and colours around the area. So do not try making an essence from a calming stone on a red surface, near other crystals, when there is healing work taking place nearby or even where arguments took place in the same room several days ago. As always, preparation of the workspace is important. If you are working indoors, physically clean the area you are going to be working in and the work surface you will be working on. Smudge the room to remove unwanted energy. If possible use a white surface to work on; even a piece of white paper or a white tablecloth will be less intrusive than other colours. Make sure the area is clear of other crystals and any other energetic influence.

Clear your mind and think about what will happen, that the natural energy of the stone will be impressed into the structure of the water. Put your selected water into a clear glass container with a wide neck, an ordinary drinking glass or jam jar is fine. Smudge the stones you have chosen and around the water; place the crystal into the water or very close to it if it does not like water. Where the stone is not placed in the water, you may want to build a grid of the required stones around the water container, four stones in the shape of a cross should be sufficient.

Place the container in the light you feel is right, such as sunlight or moonlight and leave for 24 hours. You may feel that this is too long, dowse the water and ask if enough time has elapsed and whether the water has absorbed the crystal energy. When you feel that the water is a crystal essence you will need to bottle it. The best sort of bottle is a dark colour glass, with a dropper so that you can remove small amounts at a time. Brown or dark amber glass works well, with an eyedropper cap.

The essence you now have is the Mother Tincture, your source bottle from which you can make smaller bottles of dilute essence. To do this place clean, live water in another bottle and add three or four drops of the original crystal essence. This is now a working solution and can be applied to those that need it. Crystal essences can be taken internally, but only with great care. The first important factor when deciding whether to imbibe is the water used to make the original essence and the water used to make the working solutions. These must be for human consumption and have been collected in clean food-quality containers. Second, the essence must be right for the conditions being treated.

That is a very brief overview of crystal essences. The best ones to make first are those that relate to the chakras, in particular those that can be made from quartz-based crystals such as Clear Quartz, Rose Quartz, Citrine, Amethyst, Aventurine, Carnelian and Blue Lace Agate. They are used in a similar manner to crystals, but can be applied when it is difficult to have a crystal placed on a particular part of the body, or for longer contact with the energy of the stone. A single drop of the dilute solution can be very effective and reapplied at regular intervals. If needed a small bottle can be given to the client.

Feng shui

This ancient eastern art and science is now becoming popular in the west. It is included here as there is occasionally confusion in some of the terms used. Many books on feng shui use the word crystal when they are referring to glass lead crystal, a form of glass that is used in making cut-glass drinking glasses, decanters and chandeliers. It is also used to make regular cut pieces of glass that can be hung in sunlight to generate beautiful rainbows.

Actual crystals can be used in other aspects of feng shui to assist in the movement or holding of energy. This is a very specialised area and requires the correct interpretation of the energy, its flow, the position of the building both in respect to other objects such as roads, rivers and hills and in world terms. However, intuitive use of crystals within the room, as discussed earlier, can make a difference to your house.

EXERCISES

These exercises are partly about getting to know your house and workspace and are followed by making a crystal essence. First, consider each room in your house: can the energies within each room be helped by the addition of crystals, if so what energy needs to be imparted? As you do this, log all the details in your journal, so that you can look at the rooms again in a couple of weeks and adjust the crystals accordingly. To start with, only use one or two stones.

Undertake the same exercise at your place of work. This is easier for some than others, so make the most of what you have. Again, try to notice what changes take place after you have used your crystals. This can apply to the way in which other people react as well as the way your work environment feels. If you work in a large factory or open plan office it may take longer to work or it may feel as if nothing has happened. If this is the case replace or cleanse the crystals you have used very regularly, even every day, as they will be heavily used.

Make a bag of crystals or amulet for yourself and then for someone else. If you have a friend who is going away on business or pleasure, make a travelling amulet for them. Take your time, try a certain combination of crystals and if this does not feel quite right, change it.

Next, create a Clear Quartz crystal essence as described earlier. If possible, check how the water is absorbing the crystal energy every few hours. When you feel it is ready, bottle it and then try it on yourself before giving it to anyone else. Try placing the essence on different chakras to see the effect it has, also try it over several days to get the feel of how it works. Then you may want to create a basic set for general use.

UNIT 12 – CRYSTALS AND THEIR PROPERTIES

This final unit looks at crystals and their properties. In the introduction it was mentioned that the philosophy of the book was to help the reader learn how to discern the properties of crystals for themselves, not just read about them, and it is hoped that has been achieved. As we all know there can be times when, for whatever reason, the intuitive side of our being just does not want to play. The normal reason for this is stress or illness. If this happens the stress rate is increased, as we cannot achieve what we want to, and it becomes harder and harder to use our natural talents. So in this unit you will find a list of crystals along with what I feel are their main properties. The list is there for your use, but try not to rely on it. You will have your own crystals and these may have slightly different properties, and when you work with your crystals, you may get different results. The crystals are not presented in any particular order of merit.

Clear Quartz

This is the main crystal of crystal healing, one that has many properties. Formed from silicon dioxide, it is relatively hard, with crystals of six equal sides, although in practise there are often flaws in the crystal make-up caused by external influences. It can be found in most types of formation, the most popular being single-terminated crystals of all sizes. It can also be found as double-terminated stones with one or more terminations at each end. Clear Quartz can be used in almost every situation; if you only had one stone to work with, then terminated Clear Quartz would be the best tool you could have.

There are many different shapes and types of Clear Quartz points; each type has been given certain properties and uses by some healers. In general, the basic Clear Quartz has certain attributes: transformation, transduction, storage, transference and amplification. It is also affected by pressure to generate electrical impulses and is used in devices required to make a spark or change mechanical movement into an electrical current, known as the piezo effect. On a higher plane, it is considered to aid in telepathy, connection with spiritual guides, meditation and reaching states of inner calmness. As discussed in earlier units it can be used to remove negative energy, and implant positive energy, to massage the auras and clear unwanted energy from them.

Clear Quartz is readily available and is often very beautiful and spectacular. The more you hold and look at a single crystal the more you see in it. It has been used by many civilisations throughout the world and across the ages for many purposes; it has often been bestowed with great powers and used in religious and secular ceremonies and many of the older civilisations viewed the quartz crystal with awe.

Aventurine

A member of the quartz family, but it does not normally appear in crystal shapes. This green crystal can vary in colour from pale to dark green and also comes in orange and blue forms. It normally contains mica, the sparkling gold-looking mineral. Used to assist bringing balance to an individual or situation. It covers a broad view of balancing from the various energies within an individual, their various components of mental, emotional and physical through to their male and female make-up.

It is a useful general healing stone. It can be placed in both hands of the individual or made into a grid around the treatment area. The sparking mica can provide reflection and clarity to situations, its bright metallic appearance acts as a mirror of that which is within. The green of Aventurine can be applied in the western tradition to the Heart Chakra and can provide a calming effect in cases of emotional trauma.

Amazonite

A greeny blue stone, normally obtained in tumbled form, but sometimes as a crystal. It often has white or light streaks within it. This is a wonderful stone for reducing emotional stress, without the need for traumatic release, giving the client time to assess emotional situations. It is good for the Heart Chakra and combines well with Rose Quartz or Rhodochrosite. Like Aventurine, it has balancing qualities, bringing a connection through the auric layers. An excellent meditation stone, which can produce a calming effect.

Amber

Not a true crystal, as it does not have a crystalline structure. It is fossilised tree resin and varies in colour from opaque white, through golden yellow to dark red. New sources of amber are being made available, some of which has been reconstituted. This is where small pieces of Amber are melted together, placed in moulds and finally polished. Amber has a long history of use, being considered sacred by many ancient peoples; it is readily available and can even be found on beaches. It is a protective stone, particularly for the Solar Plexus Chakra, which relates to its most common colour of golden yellow. Amber absorbs negative energy, both subtle and physical. When rubbed with certain materials Amber generates static electricity which attracts other particles. This attraction also works at the mental level, with the stone assisting in bringing into physical reality that which has been desired in the mental realms.

Amethyst

The regal quartz crystal. The colour of Amethyst is purple, and it varies from a pale lilac through to a dark, almost black purple. It is available in crystals of many sizes, clusters of crystals and as tumbled stones. A stone of great spiritual significance, which is still worn today by some religious leaders. The Amethyst is often associated with change and death. It has the transformational property of Clear Quartz, with a greater ability to help in spiritual relationships. It is a very spiritual stone and can be used to assist in meditation, bringing together the spiritual and physical bodies. It is said that the colour of Amethyst comes from red wine spilt on a Clear Quartz crystal by a drunkard, leading to another property, which is to assist with overcoming addictive behaviour. Many tumbled Amethyst stones contain White Quartz in angled bands known as chevrons. This does not take away from the properties of the Amethyst; in fact, the chevrons can be used in a similar manner to a terminated crystal when trying to direct the flow of energy, with the additional energy of White Quartz. It is also a good stone to have by the bed in cases of insomnia or nightmares, providing a safe and secure environment.

Be careful about leaving Amethyst in sunlight for too long as it may fade. Some Amethysts are created from Clear Quartz by irradiating them, but it is very abundant in the natural form.

Aquamarine

Aquamarine has long been associated with jewellery. It is part of the beryl family, which produces stones in almost every colour including the green Emerald. Aquamarine in its most precious form is clear sea blue with a sparkle from which it derives its name. It is also available in other shades of blue and varying clarity. A very useful stone as it produces many properties that appear to be generated by the appearance of the stone. It is uplifting, like a walk by the beach, bringing inspiration and clarity to mental tasks. It holds you like the buoyant ocean providing support in removing fears. It also brings feelings of care and love and can be used around the Heart or Throat Chakra to assist in expressing those feelings. Aquamarine is a useful crystal to use when making amulets or crystal travel bags.

Blue Lace Agate

A stone of light blue and white layers. It sometimes appears to be almost grey and white so be careful that there is a blue layer, otherwise it is Grey Agate. This is a stone for the Throat Chakra and very useful for throat ailments. The cooling of the blue can help reduce the redness caused by infection on any part of the body. It is, like the colour, a very gentle stone and works well with children. It can assist in bringing calm and therefore inner balance. A grid of Blue Lace Agate can provide a safe and calm haven to reach into the higher realms. Beware, as it can reduce overall temperature.

Calcite

A soft stone that comes in many different colours including orange, green, blue and red. The common form is a lump of yellow or orange calcite. This has a flowing nature combined with the energy of the sun. It provides a warming environment for growth and change. It assists individuals to look after themselves. A chakra layout can be produced from Calcite alone using the colours of the rainbow. This can produce a change in the energy of all the chakras and an increase in the flow of energy throughout the body. The flow comes from the way in which Calcite has been deposited by water.

As well as opaque Calcite, there are also crystals of Optical Calcite. These come in very pale colours and are translucent. They offer a higher level of energy and can be used to work with the spirit and higher self. Pink Optical Calcite can assist in connecting in a loving way to the higher self, opening up new avenues for personal exploration. When meditating with Optical Calcite use it to look through the ether into other realms. Beware, as the optical properties of Calcite create two images when looked through one of the planes of the crystal – you really do see double.

Carnelian

An orange to dark red quartz-based stone, which is found in forms from translucent to opaque. This is stone with feminine energy. It is a caring, warming and nurturing crystal. It has a feeling of great age about it and can help us to regain some of the early wisdom that we tend to forget. It is a stone for the Sacral Chakra, both in colour and in energy, providing a strong link to Mother Earth and, therefore, fertility. It also has the ability to assist in regaining our basic instincts and removes the chatter created by today's lifestyle.

Although well suited to the Sacral Chakra the Carnelian has a strong spiritual connection as a balance to its earth connection and can be used on many parts of the body.

Citrine

A yellow to dark brown-orange quartz. Citrine is a crystal that provides the user with a wonderful optimistic enthusiasm. Citrine comes in many shades and transparencies and Amethyst is sometimes heated to create Citrine. These heat-treated Citrine crystals tend to be closer to a darker orange colour rather than the pale yellow of the natural stone. Citrine is commonly used at the Solar Plexus Chakra where it can assist in the movement of stagnant energy. It can also help the individual to get a clearer focus on what they are doing and where they are going. The luminosity of some of the pale yellow clear crystals can be used to help bring in a connection to the spiritual part of a person. This opening of the spiritual connection can also be accompanied by great clarity of thought. Citrine is a good stone to meditate with before beginning a period of mental work.

Fluorite

A stone of higher level energies that comes in a wide range of colours and intensities. The colour range is dramatic with purples, greens, blues, yellows, reds and even clear, almost every colour under the sun. It is found in octahedron-shaped crystals, clusters of crystals and is often available in polished pieces. As it is relatively soft, it is also carved into many different shapes. A very tactile stone, it is a good one just to hold. It brings a strong connection to the higher realms, to the universe and the purity that it contains. It also brings clarity to the mental state enabling the individual to find and sort the information required, even when under stress of exams or interview. Fluorite absorbs negative energy and is one of the stones that can be used around energy-emitting equipment such as computer monitors and televisions. It sometimes needs to be used in combination with a heart stone to allow the intuition flow through the rationality of mind.

Garnet (Red)

Garnet comes in many sensuous colours of dark red to purple. It looks like a fine Bordeaux and in some ways has the same velvety feeling. Even so, it has great powers that work to energise the person. Often used on the lower part of the body to stimulate the basic energy required for life and sexuality. The energy of the Garnet is in one sense the raw energy of basic life but is tempered with an element of spirituality. Beware of using Garnet on those with high blood pressure.

Hematite

The grounding stone of grounding stones; and from its name, Hematite is also related to the blood and circulatory system and when the stone is used to draw with, it produces a reddish line. A universal helper, Hematite can assist in times of stress and trauma. This is partly because at these times we tend to lose our ability to remain grounded, which holds us safely in place. Many difficulties occur in life because at times of trauma parts of our being run away, to get away from whatever is happening, this leaves gaps in our make-up and we are not able to deal with every new situation. By using Hematite, it may be possible to hold the component parts of the individual in this plane. If a trauma or an accident occurs, place a piece of Hematite in the hands or close to the person.

During treatments, Hematite can be placed on the Base Chakra, the groin points and beneath the feet to assist in the grounding process. When working with someone who feels they have difficulty keeping in their body use a combination of Hematite, Clear Quartz and Rose Quartz to align their physical and astral bodies.

Lapis Lazuli

A blue stone containing flecks of white (Calcite) and gold (Pyrites). This active crystal assists us to make connections with our spiritual selves, guides and to help clear intuitive vision. Many people through the aeons have prized this ancient stone for its properties and its colour. Because of its age, it can help to gain a clearer picture of where one stands in relation to the universe. Although it provides clarity, it can also bring peace, as clarity can remove the problems created by fears of the unknown. Lapis is still used for jewellery and the opaque stone when polished produces an incredible depth of colour.

Moonstone

In the purist form, a pale blue-white iridescent stone. It is more often found as a pale milky cream stone. It is a stone with gentle calming properties and an affinity to the female energy. Connected closely to the emotions, it can aid in the decision-making process of the heart rather than the intellect. It brings a realisation to the individual about the natural cycles of the body and mind and is used to assist women with their hormonal cycles. Another beautiful stone to meditate with, it can take you to realms where you can bring clarity to your feelings. It is one of those stones that you want to be with forever.

Peridot

A clear bright green stone, which was very fashionable for jewellery during the 1940s. As with many green stones this is a general healer. Even in times of difficulty it can find joy and hope in the way that a sunny day brings happiness and optimism to many people. It is the green of spring and it provides the enthusiasm that spring can bring, helping people to smile at each other with a secret knowingness that there is a hidden beauty in all that surrounds them.

Rhodochrosite

A pink or pink and white stone; in gem-quality stones the pink is translucent. To some this is the stone of love. It works on all levels, physical through to astral and spiritual layers. This is a very gentle stone with an awesome ability, with the power of love to assist each person face the world and what they will find there, especially in new situations. Because of this Universal Love, Rhodochrosite brings a balance to the individual, showing them that there is a place for everything within their lives, especially themselves. A good stone for those who have not found love or who are broken hearted as it brings joy to the Heart Chakra and to the Thymus Chakra and helps to accept and give Universal Love.

Rose Quartz

The Heart Chakra crystal, a pink stone that varies from clear to opaque, dark pink to light pink. Normally found in massives or tumbled form, there are sometimes examples of small crystals available. The clear crystals provide a crisp and sharper energy. Rose Quartz is like being wrapped in a secure blanket of cotton wool. It encourages you to relax and accept peace, as well as helping to remove the pain that loss can bring. Rose Quartz also encourages people to live life, to bring their dreams into reality, in a way that only occurs when fostered by love and care. It also reminds us that there is a place in everyone's life for happiness, joy and the occasional smile and that change is good at some level, even if it is painful. Rose Quartz enables people to love themselves and to open up to other people enabling them to give and accept love.

The nature of Rose Quartz makes it perfect for single-stone type layouts. It brings the same feeling of care and love to each chakra. Because of the supportive and caring nature of the stone, it produces very pleasant feelings when placed around someone in a grid. This is a very useful and beautiful stone.

Smoky Quartz

A grey or dark brown crystal that occurs in the normal quartz forms. This is an excellent stone to assist in the grounding process and the emotional release process. A good first-aid stone as it can help with bruising and shock. As well as grounding, Smoky Quartz is supportive of change. It helps people move forward into new situations. It can help release the negative energy that stops us moving forward and attaining our purpose. At the same time, it provides protection from the negative influences that exist both externally and internally. Smoky Quartz is gentle in its actions but ensure that you are ready to take the path it may lead you along before using it.

Sodalite

An opaque dark blue stone, sometimes with white layers. A crystal of peace and tranquillity, which has sedative tendencies that calm the mind. By calming the mind, it allows the rational thoughts to take precedence over the emotional fears. Often used on the Brow Chakra, it enables the person to reduce the endless chatter that can take place in the head. In doing so, the individual recognises his or her own truth and self-esteem. Having cleared the head and increased their confidence, Sodalite helps the individual assimilate themselves into relevant societal groups.

Turquoise

The blue stone of the Americas and elsewhere. Turquoise is beautiful but often fragile, it does not like water and much of it has been treated with wax or other substances to strengthen it and to show off its brilliant colour. Natural Turquoise can appear to be pale and crumbly. Considered by many cultures as a protective and healing stone, Turquoise works on the whole body. It can be of great help when trying to reduce fevers. The colour of Turquoise relates to the Throat Chakra and can assist in bringing thoughts into verbal statements as well as with general communication. Turquoise is often veined with darker minerals and this has led to the stone being considered as spiritual, grounding and balancing. The blue is the sky, the spirit, the dark parts the earth, the grounding factor and the balance comes from the age-old interaction between the two forces. Hold a piece in your hand and feel the power that this stone can bring.

There are, of course, many hundreds of crystals, stones and metals used in healing. This small selection is given as a guide. As you work with your stones, you may find that there are other properties not mentioned, other uses and different experiences. Always use your own interpretation; it is your intuition for the situation that you are in at the time.

BIBLIOGRAPHY

The Macdonald Encyclopedia of Rocks and Minerals, London: Little Brown & Co (UK) Ltd, 1995

The Macdonald Encyclopedia of Precious Stones, London: Little Brown & Co (UK) Ltd, 1994

Andrews, Ted, *How to Heal with Color*, St Paul: Llewellyn Publications, 1993

Baer, Randall N and Baer, Vicki V, *The Crystal Connection*, San Francisco: Harper & Row, 1987

Baer, Randall N and Baer, Vicki V, *Windows of Light*, San Francisco: Harper & Row, 1984

Bentov, Ithak, *Stalking the Wild Pendulum*, Rochester: Destiny Books, 1988

Bonewitz, R A, *Cosmic Crystals*, Wellingborough: Aquarian Press, 1983

Bourgault, Luc, *The American Indian Secrets of Crystal Healing*, Cippenham: Quantum, 1997

Bowman, Catherine, *Crystal Awareness*, St Paul: Llewellyn Publications, 1996

Brennan, Barbara Anne, *Hands of Light*, New York: Bantam, 1988

Bruyere, Rosalyn L, *Wheels of Light*, New York: Fireside, 1994

Chase, P L and Pawlik, J, *The Newcastle Guide to Healing with Gemstones*, North Hollywood: Newcastle Publishing Co. Inc., 1989

Chase, P L and Pawlik, J, *The Newcastle Guide to Healing with Crystals*, North Hollywood: Newcastle Publishing Co. Inc., 1988

Collinge, William, *Subtle Energy*, London: Thorsens, 1998

Croxson, Roger, *Introduction to Crystal Reflexology*, Plymouth: Natural Solutions Through Wholism, 1997

Cunningham, Scott, *Magical Aromatherapy*, St Paul: Llewellyn Publications, 1994

Davidson, John, *Subtle Energy*, Saffron Waldon: C W Daniel Co. Limited, 1993

Dethlefsen, Thorwald, *The Challenge of Fate*, Shaftesbury: Coventure, 1979

Dethlefsen, Thorwald, *The Healing Power of Illness*, Shaftesbury: Element Books, 1983

Devereux, Paul, *Earth Memory*, London: Judy Piatkus (Publishers) Ltd, 1999

Dolfyn, *Crystal Wisdom*, Oakland: Earthspirit Inc., 1990

Eden, Donna, *Energy Medicine*, London: Judy Piatkus (Publishers) Ltd, 1999

Gardener, Joy, *Color and Crystals*, Freedom: The Crossing Press, 1988

Gerber, Richard, *Vibrational Medicine*, Sante Fe: Bear & Company, 1988

Gurudas, *Gem Elixirs and Vibrational Healing, Vol. 1*, San Rafael: Cassandra Press, 1989

Gurudas, *Gem Elixirs and Vibrational Healing, Vol. 2*, San Rafael: Cassandra Press, 1989

Harner, Michael, *The Way of the Shaman*, San Francisco: HarperSanFrancisco, 1990

Holbeche, Soozi, *The Power of Gems and Crystals*, London: Judy Piatkus (Publishers) Ltd, 1995

Judith, Anodea, *Wheels of Life*, St Paul: Llewellyn Publications, 1995

Kingston, Karen, *Creating Sacred Space with Feng Shui*, London: Judy Piatkus (Publishers) Ltd, 1996

Klinger-Omenka, Ursula, *Reiki with Gemstones*, Silver Lake: Lotus Light Publications, 1997

Kourimsky, J, *The Illustrated Encyclopedia of Minerals and Rocks*, London: The Promotional Reprint Co. Ltd, 1992

Lilly, Simon and Lilly, Sue, *Crystal Doorways*, Chieveley: Capall Bann Publishing, 1997

Lorusso, J and Glick, J, *Healing Stones*, Albuquerque: Brotherhood of Life, 1988

Lorusso, J and Glick, J, *Stratagems*, Albuquerque: Brotherhood of Life, 1987

Markham, Ursula, *Discover Crystals*, London: The Aquarian Press, 1991

Matthews, Caitlin, *Singing the Soul Back Home*, Shaftesbury: Element Books, 1995

Meadows, Kenneth, *The Medicine Way*, Shaftesbury: Element Books, 1997

Melody, *Love is in the Earth*, Wheat Ridge: Earth-Love Publishing House, 1995

Melody, *Love is in the Earth Laying-On-Of-Stones*, Richland: Earth-Love Publishing House, 1995

Ni, Hua-Ching, *Tao: The Subtle Universal Law and the Integral Way of Life*, Los Angeles: The College of Tao and Traditional Chinese Healing, 1988

O'Donoghue, Michael, *The Pocket Guide to Rocks and Minerals*, London: Parkgate Books Ltd, 1997

Ozaniec, Naomi, *The Elements of The Chakras*, Shaftesbury: Element Books Ltd, 1993

Palmer, Magda, *The Healing Power of Crystals*, London: Arrow Books Ltd, 1990

Paulson, Genevieve Lewis, *Kundalini and the Chakras*, St Paul: Llewellyn Publications, 1995

Phillips, Sue, *Crystals and Gemstones*, Plymouth: Natural Solutions Through Wholism, 1996

Raphaell, Katrina, *The Crystalline Transmission*, Sante Fe: Aurora Press, 1990

Raphaell, Katrina, *Crystal Healing*, Sante Fe: Aurora Press, 1987

Raphaell, Katrina, *Crystal Enlightenment*, Sante Fe: Aurora Press, 1985

Rendel, Peter, *Introduction to The Chakras*, Wellingborough: Aquarian Press, 1979

Richardson, Wally and Jenny & Huett, Lenora, *Spiritual Value of Gem Stones*, Marina del Rey: DeVorss and Co., 1988

von, Rohr, Ingrid S, *Harmony is the Healer*, Shaftesbury: Element Books Ltd, 1992

Schwaller de Lubicz, R A, *The Temple in Man*, Rochester: Inner Traditions International, 1977

Sheldrake, Rupert, *New Science of Life*, Rochester: Inner Traditions International, 1995

Sibley, Uma, *The Complete Crystal Book*, New York: Bantam, 1987

Sorrel, C and Sandstrom, G, *The Rocks and Minerals of the World*, London: WM Collins Sons and Co. Ltd , 1977

Stuart, J S, *The Colour Guide to Crystal Healing*, Cippenham: Quantum, 1996

Sullivan, Kevin, *The Crystal Handbook*, New York: Signet, 1987

Swan, James A (ed.), *The Power of Place*, Bath: Gateway Books, 1993

Tansley, David V, *Radionics and the Subtle Anatomy of Man*, Saffron Walden: C W Daniel Co. Ltd, 1993

Wauters, Ambika, *Journey of Self Discovery*, London: Judy Piatkus (Publishers) Ltd, 1996

Weed, Joseph J, *Psychic Energy*, Wellingborough: A Thomas and Co., 1981

West, Ruth, *Working With Your Chakras*, London: Judy Piatkus (Publishers) Ltd, 1994

Wills, Pauline, *Colour Therapy*, Shaftesbury: Element Books Ltd, 1993

INDEX

Other related titles

AROMATHERAPY

Denise Wichello Brown

What are 'essential oils'? How do they work? How can you use them to improve your health and well-being? *Teach Yourself Aromatherapy* provides a comprehensive and highly practical introduction to this increasingly popular complementary therapy.

The book covers:

- the physical, emotional and spiritual effects of essential oils
- the chemistry of essential oils
- combining aromatherapy with orthodox medicine
- the various techniques for using the oils
- detailed information on how to relieve specific medical conditions
- aromatherapy for pregnancy, childbirth, babies and children.

Denise Wichello Brown is an experienced aromatherapy and massage teacher, practitioner and writer. In this book she gives a complete, no-nonsense reference guide to aromatherapy, suitable for the general reader or for students starting their training in aromatherapy, massage or beauty therapy.

TEACH YOURSELF

BACH FLOWER REMEDIES

Stefan Ball

Bach Flower Remedies balance negative emotions and could play a key part in your journey to health and personal growth. This is a complete guide to their selection and use.

- Discover how to control and balance your emotions.
- A complete self-teach course in remedy selection.
- Full details given for all 38 plant essence remedies.
- Written by leading Bach Centre expert.
- Contents approved by the Bach Centre and the Bach International Education Programme.

Stefan Ball has written several books on the remedies and is Co-Principal of the Dr Edward Bach Foundation, which trains and registers practitioners worldwide.

TEACH YOURSELF

HOMEOPATHY

Gillian Stokes

Homeopathy is a safe and effective complement to conventional medicine for the treatment of humans and animals. *Teach Yourself Homeopathy* offers a clear and simple guide to the principles and methods of this healing art. The book provides a list of remedies suitable for home use in the treatment of minor ailments, together with guidance on how to recognise more serious ones.

The book covers:

- the history and development of homeopathy
- the selection of a remedy
- self-treatment of common ailments
- potency and dose
- consulting professional homeopathic practitioners.

Gillian Stokes is a freelance writer specialising in books on self-help and alternative therapies.

TEACH YOURSELF

YOGA

Mary Stewart

Teach Yourself Yoga explains yoga breathing and meditation with clear step-by-step instructions and illustrations showing you how to perform the poses. The book also includes a basic beginner's sequence to help you establish a daily practise routine.

Discover:

- how with regular practise and application this ancient system can transform your life
- how yoga postures and breathing promote flexibility and strength
- how yoga can relieve the stress of everyday living and bring peace of mind.

Mary Stewart has been teaching yoga for over thirty years. She is the author of five books on the subject, including one for children, and has students still practising in their eighties.